DAR AL-KALIMA
UNIVERSITY PRESS

THE SAGA OF SURVIVAL

*Armenian Palestinians, The British
Mandate and The Nakba*

Varsen Aghabekian

First Edition

THE SAGA OF SURVIVAL
Armenian Palestinians, The British Mandate and The Nakba

Author: Varsen Aghabekian

Copy right © 2023 Dar al-Kalima University Press
ISBN: 978-9950-376-52-6

Art direction : Dar al-Kalima University Press
Designer : Ingrid Anwar Khoury
Cover Drawings :Vic Lepejian

Aghabekian, Varsen
The Saga of Survival: Armenian Palestinians, The British Mandate and the Nakba
/ Varsen Aghabekian
p.175 cm.
ISBN: 978-9950-376-52-6
1. Armenians - Palestine - History   2. Armenians - History - British Mandate –
1917 - 1948   3. Palestine - History – 1948   4. Armenians - history I. Title

DS113.8. A74 A43 2023

w w w . d a r a l k a l i m a . e d u . p s

Destruction in Mamilla. The King David Hotel is in the background, 1948.
From the collection of Antranig Bakerjian.

CONTENTS

GLOSSARY

Abu (in Arabic): Father of (a name follows)

Arba Lijoch (in Amharic): Forty children

Al Samiriyyun (in Arabic): Samaritans

Babor (in Arabic): Stove

Bardizatagh (in Armenian): Garden quarter

Basturma (in Turkish): Spiced preserved meat

Bayyarah (in Arabic): Large garden/plantation

Burghul (in Arabic): Cracked wheat

Burghulgi (In Arabic, Turkish): A person who sells burghul

Chezok (in Armenian): Neutral

Dede (in Armenian): Grandfather, older man

Deir (in Arabic): Convent or monastery

Deir El Zaitouneh (in Arabic): Convent of the olive tree

Fanous (in Arabic): Lantern

Firman (in Turkish): Official decree, order or grant issued by a ruler

Garmeer Khatch (in Armenian): Red Cross

*Haganah (*in Hebrew*):* Jewish Agency underground militia

Hakourah (in Arabic): Large garden

Hammam (in Arabic): Bath or Turkish bath

Haret Al Nasara (in Arabic): Christian Quarter

Hay Yerusaghem (in Armenian): Armenian Jerusalem

Hrishtagabed (in Armenian): Holy Archangels

Intifada (in Arabic): Uprising

Kaghakatsi (in Armenian): Local of the town

Kasartilli Dahri lama Tli3na min Altalbiyyeh (in Arabic): You broke my back when we left Talbiyyeh

Kawass (in Arabic): A guard who walks in front of a procession of clergy banging a staff

Keeraj Khana (in Turkish): An area in the Armenian Convent in Jerusalem used for storage

Khashlama (in Armenian): Meat stew with cracked wheat

Kufiyye wa iqal (in Arabic): Man's headdress

Labaneh (in Arabic): Sour cream dip

Makloubeh (in Arabic translated as 'upside-down'): A traditional Middle Eastern dish

Mekaniki Armani (in Arabic): Armenian mechanic

Mekhk Hayere Lav Ormeh Chidesan: (in Armenian): Poor Armenians, haven't seen a good day

Mendz Bardez (in Armenian): Large garden, referring to the large garden in the Armenian Convent in Jerusalem

Mujaddara (in Arabic): A dish made of lentils and rice topped with fried onions

Muhalabiyyeh (in Arabic): A dessert made from milk and cornflour

Mukhtar (in Arabic): Leader of the community, village chief

Nakba (in Arabic): Catastrophe

*Nerkaght (*in Armenian*)*: Migration

*Nene (*in Armenian*):* Grandmother, older woman

Paghestiny Hayots Aghede (in Armenian): The disaster of the Armenians of Palestine

Panakhousoutune (in Armenian): Lectures

Parisiradz (in Armenian): Benevolence. Short for the Jerusalem Armenian Benevolent Union

Pergeetch (in Armenian): Salvation, the name of the Armenian Cemetery on Mt. Zion

Sab3 El Leil (in Arabic): Night wolf

Souk (in Arabic): Market

Souk Al Hussor (in Arabic): The rug market

Souk Al Qattaneen (in Arabic): The cotton market

Taifeh (in Arabic): Community, congregation

Sourp Tarkmanchats (in Armenian): Holy Translator. The name of the Armenian School in Jerusalem

Teeya seghan (in Armenian): Tea evenings

Vank (in Armenian): Convent

Vanketsi (in Armenian): Inhabitant of a convent

Vartabed (in Armenian): Priest

Vorp (in Armenian): Orphan

Wlad Alhara (in Arabic): Son of the Quarter

Zuwwar (in Arabic): Visitors, referring to survivors of the Armenian Genocide who became refugees in Jerusalem

FOREWORD

For those of us who grew up in the 1950s inside the walls of the Old City of Jerusalem, the Armenian Quarter had its special pull. It was the Quarter where our Thursday afternoon hoop rolling with the school took us to the entrance of St. Jacob's Convent (also known as St. James Convent) where we often encountered our Armenian friends and school mates. We did not know much about the Quarter and its inhabitants; the little we knew came from our class peers, Kevork and Albert. The Armenian Quarter's charm for us, the children of Palestinian Christian refugee parents after the 1948 War, was its proximity to the armistice line that separated the Old City from West Jerusalem. The thought of an Israeli sniper sitting opposite us on the imposing tower contributed to the frantic speed of our hoop rolling.

We had no idea about the inhabitants of the Quarter, the story of their lives or the hardships they had endured. What impressed our childish minds was that the Old City of Jerusalem was more than its separate quarters and the Armenian presence added a dimension that needed to be explored. This thought was reinforced later by our Armenian teachers and student peers at the College des Freres at New Gate. We never forgot how Mr. Sarkis enriched our lives as he supervised the whole school. Nor can we forget the excellence of Mr. Dikranian who taught us English in 12th grade, and who enabled me personally to pass the British GCE at an adequate level to prove my proficiency in English language.

There was much that I and other Palestinians needed to know about the Armenians and the Armenian Quarter in Jerusalem. Even when

I was at the University of Virginia and sought financial aid, I was asked if I were an Armenian. I remember saying that even though my official name, Epiphan, sounded like an Armenian name, the closest link to the Armenians of Jerusalem was the fact that my brother, Dr. Maurice, worked as the medical doctor at the Armenian clinic inside St. Jacob's Convent, and that our neighbors in the Old City, the Koutoujians, were Armenians. I received a Gulbenkian scholarship that enabled me to finish my master's thesis and that made me feel much closer to my Armenian friends and neighbors.

Varsen Aghabekian, who describes herself as a Palestinian Armenian in her autobiographical narrative published in 2021, has been earnestly researching the Armenian Quarter and its inhabitants. As someone who grew up in a Palestinian Armenian context, she had questions about the composition of the Armenian population within St. Jacob's Convent, and how the Armenian Genocide affected the dynamics between the local and incoming Armenians. She also wanted to explore the impact of the tragic events of the 1948 Arab-Israeli War on the community and its fortunes. The Armenian Quarter was in a strategic location between the opposing Arab and Jewish forces, and it was important to understand how the community had coped with the fighting around them, the resulting casualties and injuries, and the destruction of buildings and dwellings within and outside the Convent.

Sadly, the 1948 War and its aftermath led to a hemorrhage of Armenians from the Old City to greener pastures in the US and other destinations. The loss to the Armenian community resulting from the 1948 War cannot be underestimated, but the loss was for all of us in Jerusalem and Palestinian society as skilled craftsmen, artists, photographers, printers, silversmiths, teachers, and those in a host of other occupations left the city and its impoverished social, economic, and communal landscape.

One cannot be too emotional about the history of the Armenians and their presence in the Old City of Jerusalem. History teaches us that perseverance and regeneration of both individuals and communities remain possible despite wars and calamities if we contemplate the lessons and wisdom learned from studying history.

In this new book, Varsen Aghabekian does justice to an area of study and research on the Armenian community that has not been covered adequately in the past. Her love for her community and her rootedness in both the Armenian and Palestinian communities make this book far more than an historical narrative as it details the complexities of relationships within the community and with the broader society. As the book explores the past and documents the vicissitudes of Armenian life prior to the 1948 War and its aftermath, it provides a glimpse of a community that has rooted itself in the Old City of Jerusalem, and indeed in the geography of the region, with determination to start afresh while retaining memories.

I have learned so much about the Armenian Quarter and the Armenians who lived and continue to live in Saint Jacob Convent. The thirst for knowledge that I experienced as a child playing by the Convent gate in the 1950s has been quenched by this volume of love and loyalty authored by Varsen. As I read each chapter, I discovered more about the Armenians and their community in Jerusalem. I also felt growing appreciation of the many factors that make up the city of Jerusalem. Thank you Varsen Aghabekian for your labor of love and commitment.

Dr. Bernard Sabella
Jerusalem, October 22, 2022

INTRODUCTORY REMARKS

An insight of yesterday is important for understanding today, and for shaping and effecting a better future. As the daughter of an Armenian *Kaghakatsi*[1](my father) and an Armenian descendent of Armenian Genocide survivors[2] (my mother), identified by *Kaghakatsi* Armenians as *Zuwwar,*[3] I was always intrigued while growing up by the complexities of the more Arabized Palestinian Armenian orientation of my father and his family compared with the more Armenian-focused orientation of my mother's family, and how those orientations and differences interplayed and surfaced. Despite the differences, one aspect that stood out was the recollection by both my mother (1935-) and father (1923-2020), both born in Jerusalem, of the events leading to 1948, and how those events affected their larger and more extended families. That year shaped my parents' political orientation in later years, their feeling of being Armenian Palestinians, and how they raised us in a land which they both considered home.

Our interest as a family in the political developments in Palestine and our empathy with Palestinians is the natural result of our upbringing by two hard-working Armenian Palestinians who sympathized with the plight of Palestinians, and whose background (on my mother's side) as descendants of survivors of the Armenian Genocide was that of a painful history of ethnic erasure and suffering. We could not but empathize with the injustice and wrongdoing to which Palestinians have been subjected. In essence, it is a sense of solidarity with the suffering and historical convergence between Armenians and Palestinians.

Similarities can be drawn between the suffering of Armenians and of Palestinians, two indigenous peoples violently expelled from their historic homelands. Turkey refuses to accept its wrongdoing to Armenians, while Israel denies the *Nakba* of 1948[4] and continues to occupy the land and lives of Palestinians in the State of Palestine on the 1967 border.[5] My family, parents, and the rest of the extended family are also conscious of and recognize the horrors which befell Jews, the atrocities of the Holocaust, and the Jewish people's right to live in security. They always wonder why people who have suffered so much inflict pain today on others, including Armenians in the occupied State of Palestine.

There is ample literature in Armenian, but not in Arabic or another language, depicting Armenian life in Palestine. Literature on Palestine in the nineteenth and twentieth century has dwelled on the issue of Arabs, Palestinians, Jews, and the Arab-Israeli conflict. Although much has been written on the history of the war in Palestine in 1948, little is available on the impact of the war on social, religious, and humanitarian realms. Furthermore, while much has been written on the British Mandate over Palestine in general, the lives of "minorities" or ethnic groups, including Armenians in Palestine under the British Mandate, have been ignored.[6] There is even less information on Palestinian Armenians and the political events in Palestine leading to 1948, a year better known as the year of the *Nakba*.

Despite being a well-established community with an uninterrupted presence in the Holy Land since the 4th century, there is a general absence of the Armenian community in the narrative. This uninterrupted continuous presence in Palestine dates from centuries and differs from the Armenian presence elsewhere when Genocide survivors took refuge in those countries. In essence, the Armenians of Palestine have been very much an indigenous part of the population of the Holy Land since the 4th century and an important element of its mosaic, particularly of the Old City of Jerusalem.

There is some literature on the Palestinian Armenian community during the British Mandate (1917-1948) and on life under the Israeli occupation of the West Bank, the Gaza Strip, and East Jerusalem in 1967. Much less has been written on the events of 1948 and the impact on the Armenian community and the Armenian Quarter.[7] Most Arab sources on the Mandate period were written by Christian Arabs (none of them an Armenian, probably due to a language barrier). Furthermore, most of the accounts and diaries from the late Ottoman and the Mandate period were also written by non-Muslims.[8] In a nutshell, there are very few historical writings that shed light on the attitude and identity of the Armenian population of Mandatory Palestine, and the aspect of people's lives is missing from political accounts of the period. Most historiographies in the archives of the Armenian Patriarchate of Jerusalem are in Armenian. This poses a language barrier to readers and researchers, in addition to its inaccessibility.[9]

The turbulent times in Palestine, particularly in 1948, had a profound impact on the professional careers and personal trajectories of Armenians. Many opted to emigrate during the years of violence prior to 1948 or became refugees and emigrated during the following years.

Violence between the Jewish and Arab communities in Palestine grew between the 1920s and 1940s,[10] and 1947 was a decisive year that set the stage for the *Nakba*. On November 29, 1947, the United Nations General Assembly (UNGA) adopted, by a two-thirds majority, a plan to partition Palestine into a Jewish state, an Arab state, and an international zone in Jerusalem, including the holy sites. The areas which are now East and West Jerusalem (and the environs including Bethlehem) were not allocated to either the Arabs or the Jews but were to be administered as an international entity. The UN Resolution on the Partition of Palestine severed the geography of Palestine and drastically altered its spatial reality. On May 14, 1948, the British ended its Mandate over Palestine, Israel declared itself as a state with *de facto* recognition of the new state by the US, and two days later by the then Soviet Union, while the Arab Legion entered Palestine. Palestinian Christians joined Palestinian Muslims in opposing the partition and taking up arms.

The country changed rapidly, and so did the lives of Palestinian Christians and Muslims. The *Nakba* of 1948 and the loss of land by Palestinians and Arabs was a severe blow with consequences still felt today 75 years after those life-changing events. The Armenian community as citizens of Palestine was hard hit. Those most affected were the residents of Jerusalem, which had the highest concentration of Armenians in the land at the time. Both then and now, Jerusalem was one of the most vibrant and important cities of Palestine and was the city most affected throughout 1948 and its aftermath.

The common collective experience of Arabs and Armenians in 1948 in facing dispossession and the consequences of loss and displacement, brought the two closer. The writings in the *Sion* magazine of the Armenian Patriarchate of Jerusalem in 1948 and 1949 often referred to *Paghestiny Hayots Aghede* (meaning in Armenian, the disaster of the Armenians of Palestine) and echoed commentary on the *Nakba* of Palestine and Palestinians in general.

Stories told by Armenians who experienced the events of 1948 are transmitted from one generation to the other and are part of Palestine's history of dispossession, refuge, and survival. George/Kevork Hintlian conducted extensive interviews between 1965 and 1990s with Armenian Genocide survivors and his contemporaries while working at the Armenian Patriarchate of Jerusalem. He documented life in the Holy Land, particularly in Jerusalem. His work as an archivist at the Armenian Patriarchate of Jerusalem for over 30 years exposed him to a wealth of information on Armenians in the Holy

Land in the last century. His contribution to this book is invaluable and thanks to him, this book documents some of the memories of the events and personalities that shaped the course of Armenian lives in the Holy Land.

My attempt to depict the life of the Armenian community in and around 1948 is not about recreating the past or clinging onto it. It is about contributing to the overall narrative about political and socio-economic aspects of Palestine prior to the *Nakba,* and the fundamental changes which have occurred to the indigenous and uninterrupted presence of Armenians in Palestine, and somehow in the Levant in general. It is about adding to our understanding of the events of the *Nakba* that befell the population of Palestine, and the Armenians in particular. I often questioned my father, who was 25 years of age in 1948, on the lack of documentation about Palestinian Armenians in 1948, and why he himself had not documented events. His justification was:

> *"Who from the community would be documenting amid fear and ongoing battles with growing economic deterioration? Documenting was not a priority and telling the story was a challenge, especially as only a few of us grasped the magnitude of the events, the division, the collapse of Palestine, and how it already influenced or would impact our lives and the lives of the people in the region in the future. Many Armenians, especially Vanketsis, were caught up in a war and a history they were not part of and found it difficult to relate to. Only a few years before, they had arrived as a devastated people with decades of past atrocities; they were moving slowly but steadily towards rebuilding the community and were now living in their second home amid the conflicts.*

"Most of the Genocide survivors identified themselves as Armenians and Christians within religious and ethnic spheres far from politics. Kaghakatsi sympathies in general were with the Arabs ...... There was some documentation with photos here and there, but it was not systematic or adequate. Few had cameras to take photos.... the abundance of today's cameras was absent. All the events, uncertainties, the sense of injustice, defeat at times, and helplessness, I guess, were detrimental factors."[11]

Literature about 1948 and the Palestinian *Nakba* generally refer to the non-Jewish population of the Holy Land as one large homogenous group: that of 'Palestinian Arab" inclusive of Muslims, Christians, and other ethnic groups. Thus, most coverage and reference to the events rarely focus on a particular group or ethnicity inhabiting the Holy Land. Armenians then and now - although part and parcel of the larger Palestinian society and population – remain Armenians who have for centuries preserved their uniqueness as a distinct closely knit ethnic group. They are one of the several ethnic groups living in Palestine who have been affected by death, dispossession, loss of property, and the search for refuge as a result of the *Nakba* that split the Holy Land.[12] Their narrative on this period has been somehow diluted within the Christian narrative on Palestine to the detriment of documenting the uniqueness of the Armenian community and its contribution.

In 1948 and its aftermath, Armenians faced political and economic challenges just as the Arab Palestinian population did. The subsequent human and material losses amid increasing economic and political uncertainties had a long-lasting impact on the Armenian presence in the Holy Land. The period sparked a sharp fall in Christianity in the Holy Land through increased migration and the relatively small Armenian community declined. Without understanding the profound impact of 1948 on the Armenians of Palestine, no analysis of present-day Armenians in Jerusalem and in Palestine and Israel at large is complete.

This book includes five chapters: The first briefly highlights the Armenian presence in the Holy Land/Palestine. The second covers the influx of Armenian Genocide survivors into the Holy Land and the creation of a new Armenian community. The third chapter focuses on the challenges faced by the Armenian Patriarchate of Jerusalem between 1917 and 1945, the development of the Armenian community and its contribution during the Mandate years, their peaceful coexistence with others, and their lives amid rising tensions in Palestine. Chapter four describes how the Armenian Patriarchate of Jerusalem dealt with the eruption of violence and division of Palestine in 1948, the pivotal role of the Armenian Quarter, and the Patriarchate's key contribution to twentieth century Armenian-Palestinian history. The chapter sheds light on loss of property, loss of lives, the heroes of the time, displacement, disruption of livelihoods, and the second seeking of refuge by many Armenians during 1948. The final fifth chapter focuses on the aftermath of 1948 on the Armenians of Palestine.

This book has been made possible through family and other archival material, plus interviews with primary sources who lived during this period and who were able to describe the reality of Palestine. From an early age, I was exposed to discussions, readings, critical perspectives of family members and others on the Mandate period and beyond, on the fate of Palestinians in general, and on Palestinian-Israeli politics. Thus, my intention in this book is not to provide comprehensive chronological coverage of events under the British Mandate years and the situation of Armenians in 1948, but to sensitize the reader to life and experiences during such an important period. It is not a comprehensive history with extensive literary reviews, but a recollection of incidents passed on by people who lived them, or through their offspring who are a rich source of information. It is also about drawing further attention to the importance of oral history. As such, it is more of a recollection by Armenians, a people whose voices and stories in the Holy Land have been often sidelined, and of stories that are worth sharing before they are lost forever.

Prior to 1948, the Armenian community was made up of local Armenians and Genocide survivors and their descendants. It was a state of both consolidation as well as transition, with some trying to accommodate the new refugees and others moving on. This process continued through the *Nakba* period and the division of Palestine. The Armenian community in the Holy Land grew exponentially in the early 20th century due to the influx of Genocide survivors who settled in Jerusalem and environs. The community was divided between the *Kaghakatsis* and the *Vanketsis,* although both cohabited peacefully together and with other communities. They were relatively prosperous under the British administration, particularly in trade, business, and cultural activities.

The year of 1948 was a life changer for many and a period of great importance in Arab and Jewish history. It altered the geography and demography of Palestine, and Jerusalem in particular. For Armenians, the sense of "*Hay Yerusaghem*" (Armenian Jerusalem) was severely disrupted and has been ongoing to date. As such, Armenians need to record the people, places and events which were part of our lives in Palestine for future generations.

Memories, archival material, and other recollections flesh out the picture of the conditions that prevailed then. This endeavor is most essential when the context is Jerusalem – a city like no other- which has, is, and will continue to be in the limelight for its significance throughout history and its importance to many. It has long been asserted that there is no end to the Palestinian-Israeli conflict without an agreed solution on the final status of Jerusalem. Additionally, there will be no end to turbulence in the Middle East region as a whole without ending the Israeli occupation of occupied Palestinian territory and agreeing on all final status issues[13] between Israel and Palestine.

Whenever possible, and when informants and archival information were available, I tried to include anecdotes and stories which would have been lost otherwise. These stories are from informants who heard them from their parents or family members, or who experienced these events themselves at the time. Their recollections of the past are very much engrained in past events, yet intimately connected to the present in how they recall Palestine then and today. Any inaccuracies or omissions are related to my interpretation and available information as conveyed.

Armenian names are often spelled differently and I apologize for any misspelling of the many names referred to. This may be a result of my background as an Armenian whose language has been influenced by Arabic pronunciation and spelling.

There are several friends and colleagues whom I wish to thank for encouraging me to take on this endeavor. Special thanks to Kevork /George Hintlian for many hours of providing information, photographs, highlighting events, explaining, reviewing drafts, offering archival material, and leads for contacts. He assisted me with my pronunciation and spelling, and I am grateful for the conversations we held in Armenian which helped to polish my spoken Armenian.

Gratitude is due to Jirair Tutunjian for providing reference material, for sharing his personal notes collected over the years on Armenians in Jerusalem and the Holy Land, and for providing feedback on an earlier draft. Special thanks are due to Dr. Ehab Bessaiso for the many hours of discussion that encouraged me further to investigate and inject the spirit of Armenian Palestinian life into the narration, and for his review of several drafts. I am very grateful to Dr. Bernard Sabella who also provided feedback on an earlier draft and wrote the foreword to the book.

Appreciation is due to Father Koryoun Baghdasarian and Xavier Abu Eid for providing valuable feedback on earlier drafts. I am grateful to Hagop Djernazian for his willingness and support throughout data location, translation from Armenian, and for guidance in locating important documents buried within Armenian Club archives in Jerusalem.

Several people assisted in providing information or offered their time to be interviewed: Michael Genevisian, Maurice Bannayan, Mary Barsamian, Lily Ramian, John Ramian, Lucy Aghabekian, Abcar and Alice Zakarian, Vartouhi Kukeyan, Hovan Bedrossian, Dikran Bakerjian, Berj Gegekoushian, Varouj Ishkhanian, Hoppig (Yerchanig) Marashlian, David (Tavit) Terzibashian, and Marie Ohannessian. To all, I am most grateful and appreciative of their infinite patience and support offered freely.

I cannot thank enough artist Vic Lepejian for offering to design the book cover. The design reflects the two Palestinian and Armenian people sharing similar history. The Olive tree cut during the *Nakba* has an offshoot of a branch continuing life reflecting history and future of Palestine and Palestinians. The Pomegranate tree cut during the Armenian genocide has an offshoot of a branch bearing pomegranates symbolizing life and a future for Armenians. Both trees are held in palms overlooked by the wall of Jerusalem where both people will continue to live in a hope for a better life. The Church and Mosque below symbolise the unity in both history,religion and future. The design not only showcases the book but reflects the beautiful work of a talented Armenian designer who, alongside other Armenian ceramists of Jerusalem, has preserved and developed the ceramics work of their forefathers and made it synonymous with Armenians.

I am most grateful to Dar Al Kalima University in Bethlehem for offering to publish the book, with generous support from the Higher Presidential Committee for Church Affairs in Palestine.

This book is a tribute to the Armenians living through a period of time that has not been recorded sufficiently by an Armenian. It is a tribute to the many Armenians who have worked with and served Palestinian refugees in several capacities since 1948, and who have left this world while the Palestinian refugee problem remains unresolved: Ohannes Aghabekian, Antranig Bakerjian, Vahe Aghabekian, Hortanan Chillingirian, Garabed Hovsepian, Arshalous Aghabekian Zakarian, Haigouhi Aghabekian Zakarian, Apraham Toumayan, Garabet Hagopian, Mateos Kardjian, Hagop Melikian, and many nurses, physicians and other staff who worked at the Augusta Victoria Hospital and UNRWA schools and clinics serving Palestinian refugees. It is also a tribute to Armenians who worked diligently to embrace Armenian Genocide survivors as refugees in the Holy Land, and to the Genocide survivors themselves who have risen from misery to make enormous contributions to the Armenian community and the Holy Land.

The book highlights the development of the Armenian community during the British Mandate period of Palestine and the contribution of Armenians in 1948 in collectively safeguarding the Armenian Quarter. Armenians have succeeded in preserving their community in the Holy Land, specifically Jerusalem, albeit that the community is much smaller now. This is a history and narrative unknown to many

Armenians and non-Armenians. It paves the way for further analysis of the Armenian community, the Christian Palestinian community, and the Israeli-Palestinian issue in general.

For me as an Armenian Palestinian, it is a story worth writing and to the reader, hopefully, a story worth reading.

CHAPTER ONE

THE ARMENIAN PRESENCE IN THE HOLY LAND PRIOR TO THE TWENTIETH CENTURY

Indications of the Armenian presence in the Holy Land date back to the fourth century when Armenian monks, clerics and pilgrims travelled to Palestine, and some settled in Jerusalem. The Armenian presence has been revealed in architectural remains and mosaic inscriptions uncovered during excavations in Jerusalem, Nazareth, the Jericho area, and the Sinai Desert. Several of these Armenian mosaic inscriptions, dating from between the fifth and seventh century, are amongst the oldest epigraphic testimonies of the Armenian language. There are references to St. Euthymius (377-473), an Armenian hermit from Melitene/Malatya who founded monasteries in the desert in Palestine. Anastas Vartabed lists 70 Armenian churches and monasteries in the Holy Land between the fourth and seventh century. Indications of early Armenian cultural activities in the Holy Land are also reflected in numerous manuscripts.[14]

The first known monument to the Unknown Soldier is in the chapel of St. Polyeucte[15] built by Armenians in the Musrara neighborhood to the northwest of the walled city of Jerusalem.[16] In 638[17] the first Armenian Patriarchate was established and the title of the spiritual leader was elevated to Patriarch. Today he is known as the Armenian Patriarch of Jerusalem and the Armenian Apostolic Church began to appoint its own bishop in Jerusalem.

The Armenian Patriarchate refers to the area and properties centered around the St James Armenian Monastery (Convent/*Vank*) and includes the entire Armenian Quarter in the Old City of Jerusalem. It falls under the jurisdiction of the Brotherhood of St. James. The first Patriarch was Abraham (638-669).[18] Since then, there have been 97 Armenian Patriarchs in Jerusalem.[19] The St. James Cathedral, founded in the fifth century and expanded during Crusader times, is in many ways a replica of the Haghpad Cathedral in Armenia.

The oldest copy of the Armenian alphabet is in Jerusalem. Wealthy Armenian kings and queens throughout the centuries have supported the Armenian Patriarchate of Jerusalem. In earlier times, this support aided the Armenians to maintain their historical custodianship of the houses of Annas and Caiaphas, and their shared custodianship of the Church of the Holy Sepulcher, the tomb of Mary at Gethsemane, the Church of the Ascension on the Mount of Olives, and the Church of the Nativity in Bethlehem. After the Greek Orthodox and the Roman Catholic Churches, Armenians rank third in their jurisdiction over the holy sites of Jerusalem. Shared responsibility of the holy sites is enshrined in the Status Quo agreement of 1852,[20] which originated in an Ottoman *firman* on holy sites and arrangements.

The Armenian Quarter is over a thousand years old. Many acquisitions between the 16th and the 18th centuries were thanks to donations by Armenians in the diaspora and the efforts of visionary Armenian Patriarchs of Jerusalem. At the main entrance to the Armenian Convent, there is an Arabic inscription - an edict (1450) by Egyptian Sultan al Zaher Al Jaqmaq which ensures the proprietary rights of the Armenian Church and records the cancellation of certain taxes imposed on the Armenian Monastery.[21]

Beginning in 1866, donations from abroad also sponsored the publication in Jerusalem of the monthly periodical, *Sion*. In the

20th century, support from the Gulbenkian Foundation[22] largely paid for renovation work to the seminary, and maintained the physical structure and operation of the Gulbenkian library. This library is considered one of the most important in the Armenian diaspora.

The community is closely knit and has rarely exhibited clergy-laity problems, both being Armenian, unlike the other Jerusalem churches, particularly the Eastern churches in which there have been tensions between locals (Arabs) and expatriate clergy (for example, Greek). Some problems have surfaced at times within the Armenian Church over the issue of Patriarchal ascension.

Armenian chronicler Simon Lehatsi, who stayed in Jerusalem for a year (1615-1616), stated that there were only 12 Armenian families in Jerusalem. Fra Eugen Roget, a missionary who lived in the Middle East from 1632 to 1646, said the Armenians in Jerusalem were "influential and in great numbers." He added: "... of all the Orientals, the Armenians are the most zealous, most civilized and affable."[23] Arthur Hagopian[24] discovered that the oldest documents relating to Armenian *Kaghakatsis* dated back only to 1840 in the Patriarchate's 'domars' (registers) which listed births, weddings, and deaths.[25]

Under the Ottomans, Armenians comprised 23% of Jerusalem's Christians in 1690.[26] Armenians then were part of the Ottoman Palestinian fabric and Arabic was dominant in their daily communication. It is only in the British Mandate census of 1922 and of 1931 that details are given of Christians by denomination for each district of Palestine and for the whole country. In 1922, the Armenian Orthodox population totaled around 3,000 [27] and made up 4.2% of the Christian population, while Armenian Catholics totaled around 300 (0.4% of the Christian population).[28]

Armenians have deep roots in the Holy Land with an unbroken and uninterrupted presence, especially in Jerusalem. The pilgrims and monks who came to Jerusalem in the fourth century formed the nucleus of Jerusalem's Armenian community in service of their faith.[29] In the early 20th century, there was an influx of thousands of Armenians to the Middle East and Egypt as a result of the Armenian Genocide. Thousands ended up in the Holy Land, mostly in Jerusalem, and the coastal cities of Jaffa and Haifa. Jerusalem is considered the most ancient Armenian diaspora community outside the Armenian homeland. The Armenian Patriarchate of Jerusalem holds a special status with the Armenian diaspora due to its presence in the holy city, and its communal connection to the Armenian community in Jerusalem, Jaffa, and the Holy Land at large. The early 1940s were the most prosperous times for Armenians in the Holy Land and the peak of their presence. The following years were full of challenges and impediments that contributed to the decline of the community and its presence.

CHAPTER TWO

THE INFLUX OF ARMENIAN GENOCIDE SURVIVORS AND THE CREATION OF THE NEW ARMENIAN COMMUNITY IN THE HOLY LAND 1915-1948

Armenians of Palestine in Numbers

Palestine had a population of around 618,000 Muslims, 70,000 Christians, and 59,000 Jews when the Ottomans left Palestine.[30] In 1922, the population of Palestine totaled 752.048; in 1935 it was 1,308,112; and in 1946 it was 1,952.092.[31] There are conflicting statistics on the number of Armenians in the Holy Land prior to 1948 but Christians, including Armenians, made up 18% of the population. By 1925, there were about 15,000 Armenians in Palestine, concentrated mainly in Jerusalem, and with smaller numbers in Haifa and Jaffa.[32] Other figures range between 20,000 and as high as 40,000, of which it is estimated that there were 15,000-16,000 Armenians in Jerusalem. These figures are hard to verify. The two British Mandate censuses are widely acknowledged to be flawed (fear of taxation, distrust of authorities, and general fear and trauma of people).[33] Thus, accurate figures of the number of Armenians (Orthodox and Catholic) are not available. When the Mandate government conducted a census, it collected figures from the heads of religious communities. In the case of the Armenians, people who had survived the Genocide had fled their homes without any official papers, many of them orphans without parents. This made it difficult to prove identity and posed challenges to a head count.

The Armenian population in Palestine spiked due to the influx of Armenian refugees who were spared slaughter, expelled and deported from Turkey in 1915 onwards, and who astonishingly, survived the massacres and death marches inflicted upon them. Palestine was a refuge from the heinous atrocities committed against Armenians. The first wave of Genocide survivors arrived in Jerusalem from Cilicia. Twenty families followed from Adana and the number of incoming families grew to 600. By 1920, some 2,000 refugees had arrived in Jerusalem. In 1922, additional ships with Armenian orphans (816) arrived in Lydda train station via the Suez Canal. Hundreds of *vorp* (orphans) were transported from sites of their initial refuge through assistance from the AGBU, Near East relief, and the British High Commissioner in Palestine.

These survivors- mostly orphans- were accommodated in orphanages: (1) the Araradian in the Armenian Convent in Jerusalem; (2) Vaspurakan in the Greek Holy Cross Monastery for female orphans; and (3) in Nazareth for teenagers. Some were accommodated in non-Armenian church-related orphanages such as the Lutheran orphanage in Bethlehem, which had also accommodated Armenian refugees from earlier pogroms (1894-1896). A few were adopted by Armenian *Kaghatatsi* families.

Haile Selassie I, then Ethiopia's Regent, visited Jerusalem in 1924 and was very impressed by the performance of a brass band. When he found out that all 40 players were orphans of the 1915 massacres, he obtained permission from the Armenian Patriarchate of Jerusalem to adopt them. The 40 orphans moved to Addis Ababa and formed a choir known as *Arba Lijoch* "forty children". Selassie arranged for them to receive musical instruction. Along with their band leader Kevork Nalbandian, they became the first official orchestra in Ethiopia.[34] They formed the Royal Imperial Brass Band that started a tradition in modern Ethiopian music. Much impressed by the band's progress,

Selassie asked Nalbandian to compose a national anthem for Ethiopia. On November 2, 1930, the anthem was played at the coronation of Selassie I as the Emperor of Ethiopia. The Ethiopian Armenians were an intrinsic part of the origins of modern Ethiopian music, of a musical renaissance in Ethiopia that unfolded and developed throughout the next decades, and made significant contributions to Ethiopian music, culture, art, and politics.[35] The Armenian community in Ethiopia peaked at 1,200 in the 1960s. Although small in number, they played a crucial role in the modernization of Ethiopia and contributed to the development of a distinctive Ethiopian jazz. They also worked in health and served in the imperial court.[36] Today, there are around 100 Armenians residing in Ethiopia, mainly in Addis Ababa.

Communal Life, Genocide Survivors, and the Dynamics of the Armenian Community

The arrival of Genocide survivors to Palestine affected the dynamics of the Armenian community. The once-majority *Kaghakatsi* Armenians (between two to three thousand in number) who were relatively integrated into Arab society became a minority to the *Zuwwar* (visitors in Arabic as they were then called by the local Armenians) refugees from Turkey. The era is identified as one of rebirth and growth of Armenian Genocide survivors who took refuge in Palestine.

The Genocide survivors had their spoken Armenian and accent, often mixed with Turkish, which differed from the local *Kaghakatsi* accent and Arabized version of spoken Armenian. Aside from their pain and suffering, the survivors brought with them their cuisine, including the famous *Basturma*, their habits, traditions, and skills. Although many arrived with nothing, they quickly learned and mastered a skill as their source of livelihood amid general conditions of poverty and hunger. The influx of skills and skill-building despite the challenges had a huge impact on personal trajectories within the Palestinian Armenian community and beyond. The *Kaghakatsis* and the *Zuwwar,* although both of Armenian blood, were somehow distant from each other, and it took a few years before assimilation and social unity evolved.

The majority of local *Kaghakatsis* in Palestine were not affected personally by the massacres of Armenians in Turkey, but many were pained by the news of extended family members murdered in Anatolia.[37] On a positive note, some Armenian families in Palestine were elated to welcome back family members who had served in the Ottoman army, and many were elated by the victory of the Battle of Arara in 1918 and the courage of the Armenian soldiers. Some 500 Armenian volunteer fighters from around the world fought and contributed to pushing out the Ottomans during the battle in northern Palestine. A total of 23 Armenian soldiers serving with the French Armenian Legion under General Edmund Allenby were killed in the Battle of Arara.[38]

Although the waves of Armenian refugees to Palestine subsided after 1922, several Armenian families continued to settle in Palestine during the Mandate years due to epidemics and economic hardships in surrounding countries, and potential jobs in Palestine. The Armenian community of Palestine grew in the 1930s and early 1940s, especially in Jerusalem, Jaffa, and Haifa. In 1946, there was a period of Armenian repatriation to the homeland - Soviet Armenia- from Armenian communities in the diaspora. Armenians from Jerusalem joined the repatriation initiative and sailed from Haifa harbor. The repatriation of some 1260 Armenian refugees to then Soviet Armenia in 1947 had a negative effect on Armenian demographics in Palestine.[39]

Between 1925 and 1927, more Armenians arrived from Lebanon fleeing the rioting against the French, the ensuing unrest in the area, and the Great Arab Revolt. They arrived via Haifa, the nearby port of entry into Palestine, and made their way to Jaffa and Jerusalem. Other reasons for incoming migration from Lebanon included the magnetism of the Holy Land, faith and religious devotion, in addition to the development of industry in Palestinian cities and prospects of employment.

The influx of Armenians required the communal space of the Armenian Patriarchate to be expanded and the Convent was transformed into a refugee camp. Two distinct categories of the Armenian community emerged, especially in Jerusalem: the local *Kaghakatsi* Armenians living outside the Armenian Convent premises in Jerusalem, and those accommodated in the Armenian Convent (the *Vanketsis)*. Some Genocide survivors were also accommodated around the Armenian Catholic Church and Convent in the Islamic Quarter, and in several *souks* of the Old City of Jerusalem such as *Souk Al Husor* and *Souk Al Qattaneen.*

Armenians who took refuge in Palestine moved from being stateless people to being Palestinian citizens within a few years. This was possible as the British Mandate over Palestine and the Treaty of Lausanne (24 July 1923) gave Palestine a distinct nationality (Palestinian).[40] Article 30 of the Treaty stated that all Ottoman subjects who were settled on territories detached from the Ottoman Empire were to become subjects of those (new) states. In Palestine, the Treaty came into force in 1925 when the Palestinian Citizenship Order started to be implemented. The British Mandate policy of creating a national home for the Jewish people in Palestine, as per the Balfour Declaration of 1917, allowed the Jewish population to grow by regularizing immigrants and granting them Palestinian citizenship.[41] Some Armenians benefitted indirectly from this, especially those who had previously taken refuge in Syria and Lebanon. It was also possible to become a Palestinian citizen through naturalization.

By 1934, the number of Armenians in Palestine was between 15,000 and 25,000. As the political situation worsened in the mid-1940s, 1260 Armenian refugees were repatriated to Soviet Armenia.[42] It is safe to claim that in 1948, Armenians were evenly distributed in three main areas of the Holy Land: some 5,000 in the Jaffa area, 5000 in the Haifa area, and 5000 in the Jerusalem area.[43] The Armenian population of Jaffa expanded in the early 20th century and the Armenian Convent of St. Nicholas on the seafront was the first stop for Armenian pilgrims arriving by sea. Most *Kaghakatsi* lived in Jerusalem's Old City.

During the 1948 War, there was an influx of Armenians into the Armenian Quarter, mainly from Jaffa, Haifa, and the New City (West Jerusalem). In November 1948, a census conducted in both the old and new neighborhoods of Jerusalem indicated that there were 28,717 people overall in the Arab area and 85,000 in the Jewish section, including the military.[44]

The Shrinking of the Armenian Community

The shrinking of the Armenian community, particularly in Jerusalem, has been ongoing since 1948. Today, there are an estimated 1200 to 1800 Armenians in Jerusalem, with a small community in Bethlehem,[45] and about 5000 Armenians in Israel. The turbulent 1940s which culminated in the Palestinian *Nakba* triggered a substantial decrease in the Christian population as people fled the cities and towns that became part of the State of Israel. Almost two-thirds of the Palestinian population became refugees displaced internally or abroad, and the same applied to the Armenians of Palestine.

A census conducted by the Armenian Patriarchate of Jerusalem in 1948 recorded: "In the Arab section (referring to divided Jerusalem),

3000 persons, 400 in Bethlehem and a hundred in Beit Jala and Jericho. The number of Armenian refugees in Transjordan was 1500. In Jewish Jerusalem, Haifa and Jaffa, there were 1050 Armenians. Of the *Kaghakatsi* Armenian community, 529 were counted in 1948 after several families have left for Transjordan (later Hashemite Kingdom of Jordan) and Damascus.[46] According to a reliable source, between Egypt, Cyprus, Lebanon, Syria and Transjordan, there were 6500 refugees."[47] These waves of migration seriously disrupted the demographics of the Armenian population in Israel and Palestine. In Gaza, for example, there were around 15 Armenian families before 1948. After 1967 and around the late 1970s, only a handful remained. Today there is one half-Armenian family left in Gaza.[48]

Armenians have been an integral part of Palestine for centuries, not only as a spiritual community but one with vast property and assets, and with a distinct quarter that covers one-sixth of the Old City of Jerusalem. Its precious possessions, and collections of artifacts and old manuscripts gathered over centuries of presence in Palestine, makes the Armenian Patriarchate of Jerusalem one of the richest and most important Armenian institutions outside Armenia. For centuries, Armenians have not integrated into the dominant community, have preserved their mother tongue, and conduct their church services in classical Armenian. The Armenian Orthodox population decreased from 4.2% of the Christian population in 1922 to 1.1% in 1967, then rose to 3.1 % in Israel in 2017. In the West Bank, Armenians made up less than 1.0% in 2017, like their percentage in 1967. In Jerusalem, one in ten Christians was Armenian in both 1967 (10.9 %) and in 2017 (11.0 %).

Like other Christian and ethnic groups in the Holy Land, Armenians shared the territorial identity of Palestine in 1948. Those living in the West Bank and East Jerusalem became Armenians living under Jordanian rule, while those who stayed in what became Israel identified as Armenian Palestinians living in the State of Israel. This latter group was joined by Armenians who came from Russia, Armenia or other ex-Soviet Union countries in the 1990s and onwards and have become Armenian Israelis.

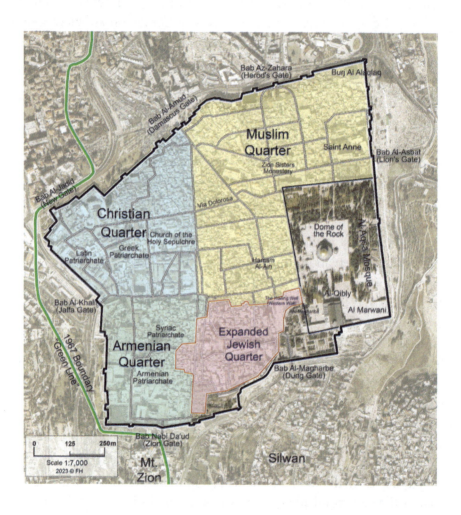

CHAPTER THREE

ARMENIAN LIFE IN THE HOLY LAND DURING THE BRITISH MANDATE

After World War I (WWI), Britain assumed control of Palestine, which became a separate territorial entity. Palestinians initially perceived the British Mandate as a savior and liberator from the Ottoman period, even though the British had a few years earlier published the Balfour Declaration of 1917 promising a homeland to the Jews. There were hopes for a new era of "progressive British rule" compared with the "despotic dark Ottoman period." However, tensions started to mount with the dramatic rise in Zionist Jewish immigration from Europe with British Mandate support and Palestinian hopes were shattered.

The Arabs sensed the imminent threat, and started to riot and strike in protest. A shift in perceptions took place with the Mandate seen as a colonial power and there was increasing anti-British sentiment. Disturbances grew until the Arab rebellion reached its height during 1936-1939. A general strike called by the Arabs in 1936 paralyzed commercial and economic activity amid general unrest and disobedience. Curfews were imposed by the Mandate authorities on Arab inhabitants and several Palestinian Arab leaders were exiled or imprisoned to quell the unrest. Arab fears and grievances were ignored. Tension between Arabs and Jews intensified, particularly over the Old City of Jerusalem where the Armenians owned substantial assets.

In 1917, British General Edmund Allenby appointed Storrs as Military Governor of Jerusalem. Storrs in his memoir wrote: *"The Armenians in Palestine were in general sober, thrifty and industrious-a good element in the population; and the standard of cleanliness and morality of their convent was higher than that of any outside the Latin Catholic, Anglican and Protestant institutions. "[49]* Although this is a positive description of Armenians, it has condescending supremacist connotations typical of a colonizer referring to the colonized.

The Armenian Patriarchate of Jerusalem: Achievements and Challenges Between 1917-1945

Throughout its presence in the Holy Land, the Armenian Patriarchate of Jerusalem was a focal point around which the Armenian Palestinian population gathered irrespective of political orientation or whether *Kaghakatsi* or *Vanketsi*. The Patriarchs were the leaders of their Armenian followers, and the Patriarchate was (to some extent still is) a major institution with political and judicial authority controlling many realms of Armenian life from the school system to cultural life, and providing subsistence support to followers in various forms. During the Mandate years, two intellectuals occupied the Patriarchal See of Jerusalem in what is considered a period of renaissance: Archbishop Yeghishe Tourian (1921-1930) and Archbishop Torkom Koushagian (1931-1939).

During this period, the Armenian Patriarchate of Jerusalem was able to regain financial stability after long years of financial challenges, particularly due to dwindling numbers of pilgrims in the early 1900s and the losses incurred due to falling overseas donations, with priority given to Genocide survivors. Several Armenian students attended theological courses at colleges run by the Church of England and upon their return, they became prominent leaders in Jerusalem and other Armenian churches worldwide.

The printing press of the Armenian Patriarchate was improved and the monthly publication *Sion* re-appeared in 1927.[50] Tourian also adapted the Armenian school curriculum to follow that of the British Certificate of Education, and supported three Armenian schools and two kindergartens in Jaffa, Haifa, and Amman.[51] During 1921-1930 there was an influx of Catholic Armenians, and the Catholic community center and church expanded to meet the spiritual, material and cultural needs of the increasing population in which Reverend Hagop Guiragossian (1930-1948), known as the reformer, played a key role.[52]

From 1917 to 1945, the Armenian Patriarchate of Jerusalem, under the leadership of the Patriarchs, worked on several fronts to make ends meet. Challenges included first and foremost the need to provide accommodation and assistance to the thousands of Genocide survivors who sought sanctuary in the Armenian Quarter. Around 10,000 Armenians who had survived the Armenian Genocide (1915-1923) sought shelter in Palestine. Some 4,000 were offered permanent accommodation in the Armenian Convent. They were housed in cells which had served for centuries as accommodation for pilgrims who sometimes stayed for several months in Jerusalem. Most of the newcomers lived in the Armenian Convent. They were given rooms with a courtyard shared by several families; under the rooms were cisterns for their use. The main challenge of Archbishop Yeghishe Tourian (also written as Turian), the Patriarch from 1921 to 1930, was to provide shelter for the refugees still arriving into the country within the walls of the monastery or outside in orphanages and monasteries.

Although many Armenians prospered during the years 1930-1945, many others were barely surviving, whether local Armenians or Genocide survivors and their descendants. Berj Gegekoushian was born in 1936 to Genocide survivors, grew up in an Armenian orphanage, and married in the Armenian Convent in 1932. His parents moved to Jaffa and later, as a family of five (parents, two daughters and Berj), returned to live in Jerusalem. They initially stayed with Abcar Cholakian (photographer) who was married to Berj's aunt, then moved to Mar Jiryes Convent (St George) in the Armenian Quarter, and afterwards back to the Armenian Convent. They returned from Jaffa to Jerusalem due to increasing unemployment and difficulty in meeting the family's needs. Berj recalls:

> *"The 1930s were hard on my parents. There was a lot of poverty, hunger, and disease. My father worked for the Sarkissian shoe business in Jaffa. In Jerusalem he worked as a shoe repairer and would walk from Jerusalem to Ramallah carrying his shoe repair box through the various villages to repair shoes. We were stricken with poverty and had the bare minimum like many others at the time. I remember playing football with other barefoot children in the convent. One of the Armenian clubs gave me a pair of shoes which I kept under my pillow for a few days before wearing them. I have seen poverty like no other. It is poverty that taught me how to take my revenge on life. I started working hard from the late 1940s until today. I opened a shop in the Carpet Market in the Old City at a very early age. It was important to help the family to survive and to show relatives that I can be equal to them and even better. I am thankful for my accomplishments. My hard work paid off and I made it despite all the challenges."[53]*

My father Ohannes Aghabekian also often spoke of the hardships in the 1930s.

> *"Times were very difficult in the 1930s. There was poverty and we had to work hard to eat. When out of school, I used to walk over 10 km to Battir[54] and bring vegetables on my back to sell in Jerusalem*

so my family would have food to eat. I was only 12 years old. We had no childhood."[55] *While I was on a visit to my uncle Chris (Khatcho) Aghabekian in the United States (US) in the early 1980s, he recalled his childhood years in Palestine: "It was so horrible that I tried hard to erase it from my memory. There was famine, loss of life, tuberculosis, and a lot of hardship. When I emigrated to the United States, I deliberately chose to forget.*"[56]

The Patriarchate helped the Armenian community at large as some families could not meet their needs. Famine in the last years of Ottoman rule, particularly in 1914, was widespread and many of the population in Palestine died from hunger. There were no longer pilgrims to donate to the monastery as Cilicia and Western Armenia were emptied of Armenians (1915-1920) and the Patriarchate lost a key source of its income. In the ensuing years, hunger and poverty were rife, and the spread of diseases such as tuberculosis, malaria, meningitis and trachoma claimed the lives of several Armenians in the mid-1930s and early 1940s. Poverty reduced people's immunity and made them more prone to infection, severe illness, and fatality.[57]

While providing shelter to Genocide survivors, the Patriarchate had to balance the solitary life and privacy required by its monks and seminarians with the presence of laity who even occupied spaces previously dedicated to monks. Furthermore, the Patriarchate had to deal with the somewhat strained relations between the local *Kaghakatsi* Armenian community and the newcomers. Although the *Kaghakatsis* welcomed Genocide survivors and even adopted several orphans, they were overwhelmed by the numbers of newcomers. There was a demographic shift in the community in favor of the newcomers and the once-majority *Kaghakatsis* quickly became a minority. The sense of the *Kaghakatsis* that the stranger

Zuwwars arriving from Turkey were taking over power from the *Kaghakatsis* (albeit insignificant) was probably profound. The rift was also a result of attitudes towards other Armenians: *Vanketsis* did not perceive *Kaghakatsis* to be pure Armenians but an Arabized Armenian community, while the *Kaghakatsis* saw the *Vanketsis* as alien to the predominant local Arab culture. In general, the Armenian community was immersed in its own issues of survival in difficult times and sought the path of least trouble.

Clanship and kinship were influential even within the *Kaghakatsi* community and divisions existed between those who had and the have-nots just like families everywhere. The *Vanketsi* community was made up of a population of orphans without parents, extended family care or guidance, and living with trauma that demanded extra efforts and intervention from the Patriarchate. One of Patriarch Tourian's priorities was to provide education to the *Kaghakatsis* and the refugee children. He replaced the old one-story girls elementary school building established in 1862, which had been damaged during the 1927 earthquake, and a kindergarten classroom located in a substandard building, with the construction of a modern school. The opening of the co-educational *Sourp Tarkmanchats* School took place in 1929. Armenian parish schools were also organized in Jaffa, Haifa, and Amman, with funding from the Patriarchate.

Education was a high priority for Armenians. In addition to the Armenian Holy Translators School, Armenian students in Jerusalem whose families could afford the tuition and fees also attended non-Armenian schools such as Bishop Gobat and St. George (British), St. Joseph and the Frères (French), and Schmidt (German). Fluent in Arabic and many with a good command of English, plus another language if attending French or German schools, the *Kaghakatsis* were generally better educated than the *Vanketsis* and held good positions in government posts and as business owners. Since the early 1900s, Armenians educated abroad had qualified as physicians and nurses.[58]

The Armenian Catholic community established around the Armenian Catholic Church[59] in the Old City was also developing. It opened two schools: the first as a kindergarten and elementary school opened in 1931 for boys only with enrollment of around 70 students (1931-1938). The second was a kindergarten and elementary school for both girls and boys (1942-1962) aiming to provide Armenian Catholics with an Armenian Christian Catholic education in which their language and culture would be preserved.[60]

The *Sourp Tarkmanchats* School became one of the best secondary schools in Jerusalem in the 1940s, and later under Jordanian-ruled Jerusalem in the 1950s and the 1960s. Unlike other non-public or missionary schools in Jerusalem at the time, the students were predominantly Armenian whereas other schools might have Jewish or Muslim/Christian Arab students. There were very few non-Armenian students, including two girls from the Dajani family who lived near Zion Gate close to the school. The school is now a shadow of its past glory because emigration over the years has reduced numbers to less than two hundred students, down from over eight hundred at its peak. This is a steep decline considering that the "graduating" kindergarten class of 1954 had sixty-four students. Former students and graduates of *Sourp Tarkmanchats* are spread throughout the world and have made substantial contributions to Armenian communities in the Middle East, Europe, Canada, Australia, and the USA.[61] Previous alumni include scientist Hampar Karagusian; philanthropist Barkev Kalaydjian; authors Kevork Hintlian, Anoush Nakashian, Vahram Mavian, Garik Basmadjian, Jirair Tutunjian, and Nahabed Melkonian; composer Ohan Durian-Khachadourian; medical doctors Gabi Kevorkian, Vartan Balian, and Karin and Talar Hagopian; economist Ohan Balian; journalist Jirair Tutunjian; teachers Arpig Kahvedjian and Nora Bedrossian; and nurses and academics Vartouhi Kukeyan, Zepure Boyadjian, Aline Balian, and Saro Nakashian.

From the Palestinian Negotiations Affairs Department (NAD) - Negotiations Support Unit (NSU) 2021.

The Patriarchate initiated several other projects. Fundraising started for the building that would become the Gulbenkian library and it was officially opened in 1932, with enormous development of its collection between 1932 and 1949. Archival documents on the fundraising efforts show that in 1929 several Armenians from Egypt, Europe, and the US donated towards its construction. Other donors included Armenians from Gaza (Hagop Arsenian) and from Haifa (Nshan Yalenezian, Karekin Gululizian, the Kevorkian brothers, Khatchig Tashjian, Levon Sarkissian, Hagop Muradian, Garabed Dadourian, Yervant Avedikian, Hagop Demirgian and Manoug Kazazzian), and from Jerusalem, Vergineh Badrigian. The bulk of the funding came from Caloust Gulbenkian.[62] The library was intended to raise the educational and cultural level of the community. Patriarch Tourian also enacted a series of reforms aimed at improving conditions within the Brotherhood.[63]

Ensuring the financial viability of the Patriarchate and securing the salaries of all Patriarchate staff remained a challenge and it was essential that the work of Patriarchate institutions was uninterrupted despite the surrounding difficult environment. Constant appeals were made to Armenians in the diaspora.[64] Berj Gegekoushian and Varouj Ishkhanian confirmed that on several occasions, staff salaries were delayed for several months. Jirair Tutunjian asserted that very few students paid tuition fees. Some of the school expenses were covered by donations from the Gulbenkian Foundation, the Armenian General Benevolent Union (AGBU), and from Armenian Americans. However, despite this assistance, there were months in the 1950s and 60s when teachers were not paid because there was no money. Everyone was waiting for the check from the Armenian American benefactors.

The Gulbenkian Library in the Armenian Convent. Photo by author.

Development and Integration of the Armenian Community During the Mandate Years

In the late 1920s, the material conditions of the Armenian community of Jerusalem began to recuperate. The Genocide survivors/newcomers to Palestine had been accommodated and the Armenian community enjoyed relative prosperity during the 1930s. The number of Armenian businesses and shops increased as the newcomers employed their skills in various vocations, along with the natural growth in *Kaghakatsi* businesses. Armenian businesses in Jerusalem included goldsmiths, silversmiths, shoemakers, tailors, tinsmiths, photography, ceramics, blacksmith, carpentry, watch repair, and foodstuffs. Their businesses were located mostly around the Armenian Patriarchate of Jerusalem, the Christian Quarter, especially along *Harat al-Nasara*, as well as outside the city walls, notably in the Jaffa Gate and Mamilla[65] areas.

Expansion outside the city walls was possible due to Ottoman reforms in the mid-1800s that permitted commercial and residential building on the hills beyond the walled city, especially in the northwest by the road to the coast. The Jaffa Gate area and its extension towards the New City in the early 20th century, became the hub of the city with banks, hotels, cafes, embassies, markets, and other businesses, several of them Armenian. The New City became synonymous with West Jerusalem and the Old City with East Jerusalem.

During WWII numerous jobs became available in Palestine in offices, canteens, clubs, military camps, and hostels. Jerusalem was full of soldiers, especially from Australia and New Zealand. Riots by Arabs opposed to the increasing Jewish presence fluctuated; the division of Palestine was soon to materialize. As soon as the war ended, the political situation in Palestine deteriorated and violence escalated to become part of daily life.

Arab opposition was growing and so was the setting up of ruthless and well-organized Jewish underground movements,[66] alongside the Jewish militia , the *Haganah*. The situation became so bad in 1946 that Jewish and Arab inhabitants stayed in their respective parts of the city. Space was shrinking and it became difficult for members of different groups to live together in the same area. Moving around in West Jerusalem was also increasingly dangerous. The King David Hotel which housed the government secretariat was blown up by Jewish militias in July 1946. Over 90 Arabs, Jews, British and Armenians were killed. Eugenie Markarian, a 29-year-old Armenian secretary and Paraghamian, an Armenian driver of a British officer, were among those killed.[67]

Despite the politically turbulent decades of the British Mandate (1920-1948), especially the latter years with unrest and ongoing disturbances throughout Palestine, and poor living conditions for many, the Armenian community underwent a tremendous social, political, economic and cultural transformation. This was especially true in Jerusalem where vibrant Armenian civil society organizations and institutions of both the *Kaghakatsis* and *Vanketsis* were established during this period.

New Armenian schools were established in Jaffa and Haifa to accommodate the descendants of Genocide survivors and the children of existing Armenian families. Several organizations were established in the early twentieth century, including unions, societies and clubs. The most important of these were: The Society of Adult Orphans (formed in 1920s); the Sion Cultural Society (1920); the Jerusalem Armenian Benevolent Union (1925); the Armenian Young Men's Society (1929); the Armenian Physical Educational Society of Palestine (1932); the Armenian Red Cross Society (1932); the Armenian General Athletic Union and Scouts (1935); Arax Armenian Catholic Society (1935); the Armenian Cultural Society of Jerusalem

(1939); and the Armenian Musical Society of Jerusalem (1939). Of these, only the Benevolent Union was *Kaghakatsi*.[68]

The Jerusalem Armenian Benevolent Union (JABU) –*Parisiradz* was founded in 1925 in the Armenian Quarter outside the Armenian Convent and was the first Armenian club to start a scouts group under the leadership of Kapriel Zakarian. Its founders included Nigoghos Bedevian, Kevork Kukeyan, Kevork Aghabekian, Yesai Kankashian, Hovannes Bannayan, Harutun Zakarian, Garabed Zakarian, Hagop Hovsepian, and Aris Dakes Soultanian. The *Parisiradz* Armenian Rhythm Band was created in the 1940s by *Wlad Alhara* (the sons of the Quarter in Arabic) composed of talented men and women without any musical training. They were the stars of most parties held at the *Parisiradz* club between the 1940s to the 1960s and played for free to generate money for the club's budget. According to the club's archives, money was used to help the needy and the poor of the Armenian community irrespective of being *Kaghakatsi* or *Vanketsi*. The band members included: Berj Ayvazian (saxophone), Setrag Soultanian (drummer), Norair (El Kawwa) (accordion), Takoug Koukeian (piano), with Fuad Mallas and Ana Baghsarian (vocalists). They were often joined by Murad Muradian, Hovsep Yeghiaian, Movses Hovsepian, Kevork Kukeyan (Kawarek) and others. In an interview, Vartouhi Kukeyan[69] confirmed what I had often heard from my father Ohannes about the *Parisiradz* assisting and providing food to needy families, especially around Christmas and Easter. The sense of community solidarity was high. This was also confirmed in an interview with Maurice Bannayan who stated that the Club elders knew all the families, what the community was going through, and the kind of assistance needed.

The Armenian Young Men's Society *(Hoyetchmen)* was established in 1929 in Jaffa and in 1937 in Jerusalem. The founders were: Haigaz Mkhalian, Aris Garabedian, Hagop Aladjadjian, Boghos Ekmekjian, and Avedis Sanjian. The *Homenetmen* was established in 1932. The Jerusalem branch was established in the Armenian Quarter before its relocation to the Mamilla neighborhood, until the outbreak of the 1948 War when it was forced to move its center to the Armenian Convent of St. James, where it remains today. Its founders were the Yergatian brothers: Levon, Mesrob and Hrayr, Tomas Vartanian, Garo Mardirossian, Krikor Chakerian, and Edward Kayayan.[70] The *Homenetmen* took pride in celebrating historical Armenian events with patriotism and zest. The Arax Catholic Armenian club was established in 1935 and its founding members included Simon Minassian (who also formed the Arax scout troup in 1960), Manuel Hassassian, Anton Sahrigian, Mihran Matossian, Vartan Der Matossian, and Anton Abadjian.[71] A Hinchagian Armenian club was also established in the late 1920s in the Christian Quarter. It was closed in 1948 with the end of the Mandate period and its members joined the *Hoyetchmen*.[72]

Armenian clubs ran scout groups, sport teams, educational activities, and programs on holidays and festivities. Their goal included the revival of the spiritual and national needs of Armenians in Palestine. There was a noticeable expansion of Armenians in sports; the *Homenetmen* Club led in soccer and boxing, and the *Hoyetchmen* distinguished itself in basketball. They competed both against each other but also against Arab, British, and Jewish teams. All-Armenian matches were covered by the local press, most notably the *Palestine Post*.[73] The *Homenetmen* soccer team proved itself among local Jewish and Arab teams as a respected competitor.

Armenian cultural societies established in the 1930s were active in lecture programs and cultural events, concerts, and music. My father often spoke of the parties and gatherings held at the JABU, which attracted Arabs, Greeks, and Armenians. Women were involved in Armenian clubs and organisations in various capacities and elected to all positions.[74] Many women were also employed in public jobs such as teachers and in the medical field.[75] In *Hoyetchmen's* 50th anniversary book (1937-1987), an editorial reflects how first-generation Genocide survivors in Jerusalem established the *Hoyetchmen* under the most critical financial conditions. Between 1938 and 1955, the *Hoyetchmen* had five heads: Antranig Markarian (1937-1938); Haigaz Mikhalian (1938-1939 and 1940-1948); Aris Garabedian (1939-1940 and 1948-1949); Sahag Kalaydjian (1949-1950); and Vartan Der Vartanian (1950-1955). They were dedicated to upholding the club's principles and presenting the Armenian community with nationalist party members who had witnessed WWII, the 1948 War, and the subsequent conflicts in 1956 and 1967. A special tribute included in the report reads: "*If one were to contemplate writing a history of the Armenian community in the latter half of the 20th century, the HEM would undoubtedly occupy a prominent place.*"[76]

The 14th Massis Scouts Group of the Parisiradz. In the back row: Vahan Aghabekian, Kevork Bennayan, Khacho Pashayan, Hagop Pabaghamian, Garabed Aghabekian, Kapriel Bedevian, Ghazaros Kaplanian, Boghos Kaplanian. Scouts in the middle row: Ghazaros Krikorian, Haig Bedevian, Kapriel Zakarian, Apraham Aghabekian, and Hovsep Khachadourian. In the front row: Yeghia Ohannessian and Yeghia Bedrossian. Photo (1930s) from the archives of the Parisiradz.

Armenians enjoyed political freedom to pursue Armenian-related political interests, to prosper economically, and to exercise communal autonomy in preserving their Armenian identity. The *Parisiradz* in particular, based outside the Convent premises and with a spacious hall, became a favorite place for parties, graduation ceremonies, bazaars, circus acts, theater presentations, and dance parties. The Armenian community educated individuals who later became world-renowned or experts in their fields.[77] Another important aspect was that the *Kaghakatsis,* most of whom had never been in Anatolia, learned a lot from the Genocide survivors about the plight of the Armenians and Armenia. Meanwhile, the Genocide survivors and their descendants learned Arabic for daily interaction with Arab Palestinians, and some learned Hebrew. English language skills were an advantage for jobs with the Mandate authorities. Thus, a pool of multilingual Armenians existed and competed well to secure public service jobs.

The more affluent Armenians moved to the new side of the city (West Jerusalem) where there were more modern and architecturally beautiful villas and residential quarters. However, many remained in poor extended family homes in the Armenian Quarter of the Old City and the walled city remained predominantly Arab (Muslim and Christian), Armenian and Greek, with a small Jewish population.

My father Ohannes (John) Aghabekian was a patriotic fourth generation Armenian Palestinian, born and raised in Palestine a few years after the Balfour Declaration. He witnessed the revolt in the 1930s and graduated from the Terra Sancta School[78] in West Jerusalem. He frequently spoke of Terra Sancta with pride and joy as one of the best schools in the region at the time and where he spent some of the best years of his life. He used to walk to and from school from his home in the Armenian Quarter, although he would often spend a few nights a week with his uncles and aunt in West Jerusalem which was closer to the school, in which his cousins were also enrolled. His upper school years were often interrupted due to increasing tensions between 1937 and 1944. He graduated in 1942, a few years before the school closed in West Jerusalem. Despite his family's financial difficulties, his dream was to graduate from Terra Sancta. Thankfully he was able to do so with help from his maternal uncles and aunt, and he knew that upon graduation his fluency in English would enable him to find a job easily.

My father and other Armenian, Arab Palestinian and Jewish men and women worked for the British Mandate in Palestine in civilian jobs such as clerical work, the postal service, and in the foreign office. My father was released from his post on May 15, 1948, as the Mandate was coming to an end. We often teased him that he worked with the British Mandate that enabled the Balfour promise to materialize but my father would ignore the comment, pretend he did not hear us, or even blush when he was much older. He often justified his work as a necessity due to the dire economic situation at the time and the fact that jobs in the public sector were available. He also stressed that it was not perceived in a negative light to work for the British Mandate at that time, especially in the earlier years. These employees worked for the Mandate over Palestine and held Palestinian passports. Knowing his personality, I believe that my father would have been dissatisfied, especially in the latter years of the Mandate.

My father lived through the 1948 division of Palestine and experienced the uprooting and dispossession of several of his family members, both from his maternal and paternal sides, from West to East Jerusalem, turning from being property owners to being destitute. He later worked with Palestinian refugees as a young teacher in refugee camps in Jericho, worked with UNRWA in Amman and Beirut, returned to Jerusalem in 1963, lived through the 1967 War, and continued to work with UNRWA for another 20 years serving Palestinian refugees, alongside several other Armenians.

My father's marriage in 1956 to a descendent of two Armenian Genocide survivors gave him an additional perspective on displacement, trauma, and the suffering that transcends generations. He had to understand and appreciate the ongoing trauma of his parents-in-law as Genocide survivors and the transgenerational trauma of my mother and her siblings. In addition, my grandfather lost his blacksmith's workshop in West Jerusalem in 1948 and my father was obliged to extend assistance to family members in need. He often spoke about 1948 with bitterness as the year that *"started the breaking of his extended family's presence in Palestine and added to everyone's suffering and trauma."* To my father, life was not the same after 1948.

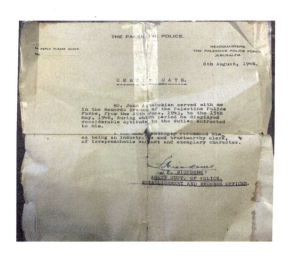

John Aghabekian's work release certificate from the Palestine Police 1948 (family archive).

Many Palestinians worked in the offices and services of the British Mandate, including a disproportionately large number of Christians. In 1921, there were 2751 civil servants in Palestine: 1338 Christians, 719 Muslims, and 514 Jews.[79] It is said that over 150 Armenians in Jerusalem alone were working for the public services of the British

Mandate.[80] The Zakarian family had several family members working for the Mandate Authority in Palestine. Ivan (Yervant) Zakarian had worked for the British/Palestinian authorities in Tulkarem and was responsible for the municipal water supply, the railway, and schools. His brothers Victor and William both worked with the British Mandate and left for Britain after 1948. Paul Zakarian was also a government officer and his sister Isabelle worked at the department that issued passports. Apraham Gazmararian and others worked at the Jerusalem health department.[81] Krikor Krikorian was Deputy Chief Medical Officer for Palestine.[82] Vahan Kalbian was the private physician of the High Commissioner and his official guests. Employment with the Mandate authority invariably increased interaction among the various ethnic and religious groups, whether while on duty or informally afterwards.

> *"We shared the same offices with often Arabs, Christians, Muslims, Jews, Armenians, Greeks, men and women. We sometimes had coffee in cafes after work or attended activities in the evenings. My uncles had business friends from both sides, Arab and Jewish."[83]*

Other prominent Armenians include Khasho Effendi Kankashian who was appointed by the High Commissioner as a member of five official and non-official assessment committees on the Urban Property Tax;[84] advocate Hovannes Merguerian practiced for over sixty years; Hovsep Krikorian worked at the port in Jaffa; Hovhannes Donabedian worked as an engineer for the British Government of Palestine in the Department of Public Works. Others included Apraham Tutunjian who was telephone installer and telephone lineman, Hanna Nazar (Bannayan) a photographer, Puzant Semerdjian and Sahag Genevesian at the health department and Nazig Mnatzaganian and Hagop Paraghamian.[85]

Once it became apparent that they could not return to their former homes, the *Vanketsis,* the destitute survivors of the Armenian Genocide who came to Palestine in the early 1920s, focused on reconstructing their shattered lives and building their community in Palestine. Although coping with their intergenerational trauma as survivors and descendants of the Genocide, they gradually prospered as craftsmen in various vocations. Armenian social and cultural life in general was very much organized through the efforts of paterfamilias (clan heads) and the young educated, multilingual generation grew rapidly.

A few romantic relationships between members of the Palestine Mandate forces and Armenian women ended in marriage and around 15 Armenian women married English servicemen. Anna Chillingirian Marashlian married Arthur Harris; Sopheeg Kaplanian married Jim Toon; Takoug Hovsepian and Takoug Bannayan married British servicemen; Mariam Toumayan married John Mitchel; and Anna Toumayan married Charles Harbon. (Charles spoke Arabic, served in Jenin (a city in the north of the West Bank) and became the driver of the High Commissioner.)[86] Once British service men were evacuated, the Armenian wives accompanied their husbands to Britain after a short stay in Egypt.

The Armenian Patriarchate of Jerusalem had held jurisdiction over Armenians in Palestine, Southern Syria, Lebanon, Cyprus, and Egypt. Under the British Mandate, its authority included Palestine and Transjordan. One of the main disagreements between the Patriarchate and the Armenian community occurred in 1930 during the British Mandate when the Mandate authority favored that the patriarchal election be held exclusively in the Brotherhood's General Assembly/ Synod, which comprised elected clerics of the St James Brotherhood and was presided over by the Patriarch. This eliminated the previous national character of the election where *Kaghakatsis* were traditionally given a chance to voice a preference (although not necessarily accepted).

Thus, the Armenian people were excluded from voicing their opinion. This was opposed mostly by the *Kaghakatsi* community; the *Vanketsi* community were preoccupied with their survival and restricted by their lives within the walls of the Patriarchate and the Monastery. The situation was generally seen as grave interference by the Mandate in the affairs of the Patriarchate and it had a far reaching impact still felt today.[87] The disappearance of a voice or even the superficial engagement of the laity could allow the Patriarchate to oversee its vast real estate holdings without oversight from any other entity. The diminishing traditional role of the community has invariably paved the way for potential mismanagement.

Armenian figures used to visit the Patriarch in his summer residence at Baron Deir in Bethlehem, also known as the Armenian Palace. It also served as a spiritual retreat and recreational site for centuries where Armenian families could picnic and socialize. The olive trees provided oil and olives to the Patriarchate.[88] These were times when the community was able to informally interact with the Patriarch, and the visits were awaited and enjoyed by many.[89]

A gathering of Armenian dignitaries at the Patriarch's summer residence at Baron Deir. In the first row, second from the right is Fr. Haigasoon Aprahamian; fourth from the right is Patriarch Israelian; to his right is Dr. Vahan Kalbian: and the last person on the first row is Parsekh Guderian. In the second row, the first from the right is Bedros Hintlian and the third from the right is his business partner Hanna Tabourian. The first from the left on the second row is Murad Manougian and sitting next to him is Satenig Kalbian né Torossian (the wife of Dr. Kalbian). In the third row at the back, the second from the right is Garbis Hintlian sitting next to his sister Sultanig Manougian. Photo taken around the mid-1940s and provided by Kevork Hintlian.

Reflection on Coexistence

Overall, relations between the Armenians and Arabs and Jews were cordial but there were mounting tensions in the years leading up to 1946. I often heard my father and his cousin Hortanan Chillingirian (Marashlian) speak of my grandparent's Jewish neighbors in the Old City. It was the family of Rabbi Weingarten, head of the Jewish community and resident of the Jewish Quarter, who lived directly next to my grandparents in the Armenian Quarter.[90] My aunts and grandmother often communicated with his daughters and wife through the windows of the room or the roof. It was coexistence at its best and transcended politics, but it was soon to be shattered. My father often iterated that:

> *"Generally, people had little but coexisted rather peacefully. Our Armenian Hay Yerusaghem (referring to the Armenian Quarter) was relatively prosperous and lively. We had good neighborly relations in the Old City. Arabs and Armenians were living very close to the Jewish Quarter. We often greeted each other and moved through the four quarters with ease. Armenians and Arabs would go to Jewish homes and kindle the oil lamps which Jews could not light on the Sabbath. We bought from each other and exchanged food and sweets during feasts and on ordinary days. We would frequent the same restaurants, cafes, cinema and stores flourishing on the new side of the city. Encounters and relationships weakened with the partition in 1947, and the increasing activities of the Haganah and mounting suspicions of the other. The once mostly religious Jewish community in the Jewish Quarter was becoming more political and our interaction weakened by the day as insecurities*

increased. The social and human interaction soon disintegrated." [91]

Vartouhi Kukeyan recalled: *"My father as young as seven years old was called to kindle oil lamps at Jewish neighbors' homes. He often mentioned doing so for Rochella who used to give him pastry made with honey, which he expected to get every time he helped Rochella with the lamps."[92]*

Armenian *Kaghakatsis* frequented Jewish dressmakers in the Jewish Quarter. There were also a few marriages with Jews. For example, Khachig Kukeyan was with a Jewish woman for two years and had a son with her. Ohannes Kukeyan was a hairdresser at the King David Hotel and was going out with a Jewish woman called Rifka. In 1948, she remained on the west side of Jerusalem while he remained on the east side. Kukeyan later left for Egypt and married a Greek woman. This trend of Jewish-Armenian romantic relations existed, albeit not to a large extent, but was more of Armenian men with Jewish women rather than vice versa.[93] There was a similar trend at the time of Armenian-Christian Arab marriages, and a few Armenian-Muslim Arab marriages, albeit among the *Kaghakatsis* and not the *Vanketsis*. Mixed marriages were not welcomed and the preference continued to be for endogamous community marriages.

My paternal grandparents' house was located at the southern end of the Armenian Quarter, bordering the Weingarten's Jewish residence, and with a Muslim Arab house (the Nammari family) sandwiched between my grandparents' house and my fathers' maternal uncles in the Banayan courtyard. This was the reality of cohabitation with day-to-day communal interactions. The Armenian Quarter was full of Armenian residents, as were the other quarters of the Old City with their respective communities and some mixing of groups here and there.

Although there were communal boundaries based on ethnicity and religion in the Old City, in Ottoman times some mixing allowed for the forging of ties between Muslims, Christians and Jews who shared courtyards and daily life, and even had mixed musicians performing at weddings. The separation and identification of quarters along sectarian lines in Jerusalem with the division of four quarters became pronounced in the mid-19th century, although the census of 1905 showed Muslims living in the Jewish Quarter and Jews living in the Muslim Quarter.[94]

The Aghabekian house in the Armenian Quarter with one of its rooms on top of the arch. On the left is the window of what was the Weingarten's house.
Photo by author.

The spirit of interpersonal conciliation and brotherhood existed as people rejoiced, entertained, and celebrated together. The Greek and Armenian communities, for example, hosted celebrations in which they opened their respective patriarchates to the public and offered refreshments. Relations with Jews started to cool with the immigration of new Jews during the early Mandate years and onwards.[95]

In general, our elders express satisfaction with those simple lives despite the poor economic conditions. My maternal grandparents who survived the Genocide were grateful to be alive and moving forward. They were grateful to make friends with other Armenian families whom they considered as family in the absence of their blood-related family members, as both grandparents were orphaned at a very young age. My parental grandparents, on the other hand, were very much part of a larger well-established *Kaghakatsi* clan with a certain degree of power in their community. Despite all the hardships, the Armenian community prospered during the Mandate years, with some individuals in particular becoming prominent locally and later, internationally.

The *Kaghakatsis* traditionally had strong relations with the Arabs and these grew stronger with both the *Kaghakatsis* and the *Vanketsis* over time. Cordial relations existed, especially with the Muslim Jaouni and Dajani families just outside the Nabi Daoud (Zion Gate). The Al Dissi and the Bashiti families were also neighbors and had daily interaction with the Armenian community. There were some business partnerships between Armenians and Palestinian Arab Christians before 1948 and these continued after 1948, including the Arsenian and Hanania pharmacy, Melikian and Hannush (general merchants and commission agents), and the fashion store of Ghazarian and Hindieh.

Generally, Christian communities had amicable relations with other communities. In Jerusalem, the Muslim Khalidi family had a strong relationship with the Greek Orthodox while the Muslim Dajanis had a strong relationship with the Armenians. These relationships where significant for settling disputes, mediation, and business partnerships.[96]

The elders in my family always boasted about having strong ties with everyone. They often referred to the good old days of the past. They perceived their life at that time, despite all the challenges, as much simpler and less complicated. *Nene* Naze (my father's maternal aunt married to my paternal grandfather's cousin- an Aghabekian) often spoke about her family's close relationship with the Husseinis (a prominent Palestinian family) and the times they spent together in Jerusalem and Jericho. She spoke a lot about the good times spent at the *bayyarah* (garden). The closeness was confirmed to me years later in the 1980s by the late Dr. Salim Al Husseini who was working with my father at UNRWA and who knew *Nene* Naze. He mentioned several Armenian cooks and nannies who had worked for the Husseini family. Dr. Husseini himself had picked up several Armenian words which he repeated to show the relationship. *Nene* Naze's daughters Arshalous and Haigouhi lived into their late 90s and were long-time friends with Zuleikha Shihabi and Haifa Khalida. They frequently spent winters together in Jericho.

Arabs and Armenian *Kaghakatsis* attended each other's weddings and other joyful events where people mixed. Armenian weddings were times of joy and celebration with scout groups leading the couple to church and surrounded by most of the community members who were like a one big family. The *Kaghakatsi* were, in fact, a big family as most were related in one way or another. Marriage within the *Kaghakatsi* community was prevalent and favored.

The wedding of Antranig Bakerjian and Nectar Bannayan (1944). Nectar was my father's maternal cousin. From family archives. Photo provided by Dikran Bakerjian.

Several Armenians had stores or were street vendors in the Old City markets next to Arabs and developed friendships as neighbors, merchants, and vendors. This daily interaction helped Armenian survivors of the Genocide to develop their Arabic language, albeit spoken with a distinct accent which characterized *Vanketsi* Arabic-speaking Armenians.

Photo provided by Maurice Bannayan. From right to left: Gabi Aprahamian,
Eugenie Aghabekian, Hagop Zakarian, Haigouhi Aghabekian, Arshalous
Aghabekian, Vahe Aghabekian, and Berj Aprahamian. Photo of a Parisiradz party
in the 1940s.

Memories of Armenian life before 1948 include a cosmopolitan Jerusalem with vibrant institutions, religious celebrations, demographic diversity, a British and other international presence, expansion of the New City, mostly towards West Jerusalem and the outskirts of the Old City in Sheikh Jarrah. Armenians dedicated themselves to hard work, especially those who needed to establish themselves in their new home. There were strong family ties and communal collective work; some left school to work as wage laborers to provide for their families or were apprentices in workshops to train for a future vocation or career. Several Armenians opened small stores to meet family needs.

Varouj Ishkhanian recalls: *"My father had a small place in the Old City where he fixed the one-head burners (babor in Arabic) widely used then for cooking. At the same time, he was responsible for lighting the oil lamp (fawanees-fanous singular) streetlights in the Old City at sunset and putting them out at sunrise. At the young age of 13, I used to carry a box and sell cigarettes to the Jordanian army around New Gate. Later, I was an apprentice in an Armenian-run photography studio (Semerjian) and was paid very little. I earned more when I was selling cigarettes, but I learned the basics to help me move later to my own photography work. Those were the best years despite all the odds. People were much nicer, kinder, and purer."* [97]

Armenian engagement in politics was slight compared to their socioeconomic contribution. They maintained neutrality in the divisive and volatile Jewish/Arab conflict to avoid provoking any group.[98] Armenians were not part of the Muslim-Christian Associations created to demonstrate opposition to the Balfour Declaration on its first anniversary. These later became key representatives of the local Arab Palestinian population, especially in the early Mandate period. The Arab Higher Committee established later included several Christians in key positions but no Armenians. Furthermore, Armenians were not employed in Arab Palestinian newspapers established before or during the British Mandate many of which belonged to Palestinian Christians: *Filastin,* owned by the Al Issa family; Jurgi Hanania (*Al Quds*); Mushahwar and Khoury (*Al Insaf*); Emile Alonzo (*Al-Taraqqi*); Khalil Beidas's political weekly in Haifa; and Wahbeh Tamari's weekly in Jaffa.[99]

Within the *Kaghakatsi* community, there was strong sympathy towards Palestinian Arabs with whom they shared a long history of harmonious coexistence and a shared culture. In political terms though, especially among the *Vanketsis*, the belief was that any political involvement should serve Armenian political interests and be detached from the increasing bitter political quarrels between the Jews and the Arabs in Palestine. I have heard stories from my father and relatives that, during 1948, Armenians mainly acted as neutral human beings who cared for people's lives irrespective of whether they were Jew or Arab. There are stories told of families protecting Arabs and Jews alike who sought shelter or safety. Yet, my father often spoke of sympathy and empathy towards Palestinian Arabs, especially from 1946 onwards with the partition of Palestine and the refugee problem, including that of Armenians. It was no longer possible for Armenians to remain onlookers with indifference and distance from what was taking place.

While a few Armenians may have actively joined the resistance and the struggle against colonialism, the majority did not actively participate in demonstrations or military acts. Armenians' main concern was to strengthen the Armenian community, rehabilitate mentally after the horrors of the Genocide, accommodate the newcomers, and put food on their table. Nevertheless, their presence in a conflict-ridden area subjected them to violence, curfews, unemployment, food scarcity, killings, and other disruptions of life similar to the larger population of Palestine.[100] The years 1947-1948 remain a period with an everlasting impact on everyone in the region and represent devastation, fear, humiliation, violence, loss, bitterness, poverty, uncertainty, and feelings of injustice.[101]

Contribution of Armenian Palestinians during the British Mandate Years

One may confidently assert that Armenians contributed to the enrichment and development of the country throughout the Mandate years and onwards in all facets of life. For many, the years were transformative. Armenians mastered diverse occupational crafts and were pioneers in introducing these crafts to Palestine.

The master ceramists Ohannessian, Balian and Karakashian, from three prominent Armenian families from Kutahya, came to Palestine to work on the restoration of the tiles of the Dome of the Rock. They introduced ceramic work to Palestine in 1919 in a workshop in the Muslim Quarter and opened ceramics workshops employing and training hundreds of young Palestinians and Armenians. Beautiful tiles that decorate the old homes and villas of West Jerusalem abandoned by Palestinians in 1948 were the work of these Armenian ceramists. They introduced Armenian pottery to Jerusalem where it had not existed previously.[102]

Armenian merchants prospered, including: Megerditch Kaplanian, Garabed Zakarian, Boghos Merguerian, Kevork Merguerian, Hovannes Gazmararian, flour merchant Vahan Baghsarian, cracked wheat merchant Kalaydjian, and the Sawabinis (Genevisians) who made aromatic soap.[103] Two of the largest factories in Palestine were opened in the 1930s: the Ohanessian factory for paper and the Mardirossian chocolate factory. Armenians dominated as goldsmiths during the Mandate years and later. After the earthquake and destruction of parts of their market in the Old City, most moved to the Dabbagha where one area was known as "The Armenian Goldsmiths Market" according to a sign in English, Arabic, and Armenian.

Several Armenians worked in banking and in Barclays Bank. Some continued to work with Barclays even after seeking refuge abroad.[104]

Shoemaking and shoe stores were also Armenian niche crafts during the Mandate years. Arshag and Khatchig Sarkissian (both orphans and survivors of the Genocide) had a shoe factory and two retail outlets in Jaffa with over 50 employees.[105] Hovsep Garabedian was a well-known shoemaker in West Jerusalem.[106] Other prominent craftsmen of the last century included Boghos Kaplanian, Hagop Krikorian, Tateos Tateossian, Krikor Mnatzaganian, and Kevork Kaplanian.[107] Hagop Bekarian was a shoemaker in Jerusalem up until 1948, while G. Manjikian and W. Sarkissian had a shoe store in Haifa.

Armenians were some of the first trained medical staff during the Mandate years. Ashkhen Ohannesian; Annig Minassian (an orphan Genocide survivor and midwife who probably attended the births of most of the children born in Qalqilia from 1940-1967); the Barkho sisters (Shoushan, Manoushag and Arousiag) worked at the Augusta Victoria Hospital (AVH) on the Mount of Olives; Louey from Aleppo worked as a nurse in Jaffa but moved to AVH after 1948 and was the nurse in charge of the surgical ward; Mary Kahkedjian Franji[108] (a well-known nurse in the Old City who worked at the Spafford Center in the Muslim Quarter); Vehanoush Aivazian was a nurse in Ramleh; Hripsimeh Surtukian was chief nurse at the hospice; and Mary Tutunjian was a nurse in Jerusalem. All were trained during the British Mandate years and mentored several Palestinian nurses. Ani Sipilian was educated abroad and was an anesthetist at AVH, while Siroon Der Vartanian was a graduate in nursing from the AUB and worked at AVH and the Spafford baby home in Jerusalem. Ani Sipilian's and Siroon Der Vartanian's pursuit of studies outside Palestine, alongside other Armenians such as Nevart Yaghlian, highlights appreciation at the time of higher education as a tool for advancement.

Armenian photographers continued to dominate this field following the introduction of photography to Palestine by Yesayi Garabedian[109] in the 1850s. More Armenian studios were opened, and Armenian and non-Armenian apprentices were trained. The work of Armenian photographers during the Mandate period and immediately afterwards was of the utmost importance and they monopolized photography in Palestine during the 20th century. Their work portrayed life during

Kegham
Daghilian
Elia
Kahvedjian

various periods of turbulence and several Armenian photographers are credited for depicting social and political developments before, during, and after 1948. These photographers include Kegham Daghilian who moved from Jaffa to Gaza and documented the post-1948 refugee camps around the suburbs of Gaza. Hrant Nakashian was also instrumental in portraying life in refugee camps in Gaza and many of his photos are still used today in material referring to that period. Nakashian, a descendent of Genocide survivors, grew up in Jaffa where he opened his first studio, Venus. He was forced to leave his studio during the *Nakba* and settled in Gaza, where he opened Studio Hrant. He worked for the United Nations Relief and Works Agency (UNRWA) and the United Nations Emergency Force (UNEF). His photos have been identified as the most illustrative and complete in their depiction of the details of the daily lives of refugees and are a distinguished resource on Palestinian suffering.

Elia Kahvedjian found permanent sanctuary in Jerusalem after his ordeal as a Genocide survivor and became one of the most prominent photographers in the Holy Land during a 60-year period despite several wars. The photographs shot from the mid-1920s to the mid-1960s continue to be sold today. He was in contact with famous military figures such as Glubb Pasha, the founder of the Arab Legion; Dame Kathleen Kenyon, the prominent archeologist of Palestine; Pere Roland de Vaux of the Ecole Biblique; Dutch archeologists; judges; and celebrities visiting Jerusalem. During the Second World War, besides running his Elia Photo Service, he documented the restoration of holy sites, including the Holy Sepulcher.[110]

Armenians Amid Turbulent Years in Palestine

The 1940s presented new challenges to Armenians as tensions and hostilities between Palestinian Arabs and Jews grew, especially in 1946 and onwards. This was coupled with increased Jewish immigration to Palestine. The Armenian community was cautious not to take sides but also could not remain onlookers. Fearful of increasing violence, a few Armenian families started moving abroad in the early 1940s. Some left to countries in the region, and a few to Europe and the US. For Armenians who emigrated in the early 1940s or later due to the 1948 War, or who were internally displaced, integration was much easier than for their forefathers as refugees from the Armenian Genocide. Armenians were more integrated in sentiment and in practice with the societies around them and shared a sense of common destiny.

Armenians have suffered politically, socially, and economically like Palestinians, including the loss of their properties in 1948. A look at the years before, during and after 1948 reflect Armenian engagement as part and parcel of the larger Palestinian Arab community and their courageous efforts to prevent the occupation of the Old City by defending Jaffa Gate. The community lost around forty members in 1948 with some 400 wounded. Some *Kaghakatsi* Armenians who had not experienced seeking refuge from the Armenian Genocide became refugees for the first time when they were displaced from West to East Jerusalem. Some Armenian survivors of the Genocide who had settled in Palestine became refugees for a second time in less than 40 years. Those who came to Palestine as orphaned children and adolescents from the Genocide were adults in the 1940s, many of them with families. They became refugees displaced from Haifa and Jaffa, for example, and taking refuge in East Jerusalem, Lebanon, Jordan, and Cyprus. It is believed that the Armenian population in Lebanon increased noticeably after the Palestinian *Nakba*.

In a phone interview in 2022 with Mary Kouyoumdjian Barsamian, an 86-year-old Armenian American born in 1936 in Jerusalem and living in Cleveland Ohio, USA, she stated:

"My father Nazaret (a Genocide survivor) grew up in an orphanage in Jerusalem and moved with his family to Amman in 1945, along with his two brothers Kevork and Aharon Koyoumdjian. He used to make suits for the army. My memories of 1948 as a 13-year-old include Armenians fleeing from the west to the east of the River Jordan and taking refuge in the Al Ashrafiyeh area where Armenians were concentrated. The Armenian school was packed with refugees and so was the Homenetmen club. Several Armenian families, including mine, accommodated fleeing Armenian families. I vividly remember hearing the shelling of various public facilities as far away as Amman. When my mother passed away, my father remarried a Jerusalemite from the Der Hovannessian family, and they lived in Jerusalem for some years. I and my two brothers emigrated to the US in the 1950s. My father passed away in 1964 and his second wife and children joined us in the US in the 1960s. The family of the woman who became my sister-in-law also left Jaffa to settle in Amman in 1946/47. They also emigrated later to the US. Many Armenian families left Amman and Jerusalem for a safer place with more opportunities. Several of my family members and their descendants have ended up in the US."

Displacement from West to East Jerusalem.

Displaced from Haifa and Jaffa East Jerusalem, Lebanon, Jordan, and Cyprus

Members of the Hoyetchmen club during Christmas in the Kirachkhana
(Keeraj Khana) in 1947.
Photo from the Hoyetchmen's 70th anniversary book.

Members of the executive committee of Hoyetchmen sitting in the first row.
Graduates of the Armenian school in the second and third rows. The picture
is from the annual gathering of Armenian graduates 1947. Photo from the
Hoyetchmen's 70th anniversary book.

CHAPTER FOUR

THE CHURCH, COMMUNITY, THE 1948 WAR AND ITS EFFECT ON ARMENIANS OF PALESTINE

The Armenian Patriarchate was instrumental throughout the 20th century in holding the Armenian Church and community together during difficult times. It enabled Armenians to survive and dealt with religious, educational, cultural, ecumenical, and governmental matters. At critical junctures, the Patriarchate was responsible for almost everything: securing the lives of the community, feeding people, providing shelter, and offering daily services in the style of a mini municipality.

Successive Patriarchs played the roles of clergy, diplomats, managers, and community organizers in a volatile environment plagued with ongoing conflict. They rose to the challenge of remaining steadfast and surviving, keeping the community together, and preserving Armenian cultural heritage in the Holy Land. They were religious and political leaders who served the physical, mental, and spiritual needs of the community. The years around 1948 were very challenging to both the Church and the laity, and changed the lives of Armenian Palestinians.

The Period from 1945 to 1949

From 1945 to 1949, the Patriarchate faced numerous challenges, most notably its responsibility to maintain neutrality and not interfere in political developments in a land of conflict. Since the Armenian

Patriarchate of Jerusalem holds responsibilities in various areas under different jurisdictions, it is obliged to maintain amicable relations with the government authorities and religious communities of all faiths. This always necessitates careful and measured diplomacy. In 1948, the Patriarchate had to deal with the results of the intensifying conflict between Palestinian Arabs and Jews that culminated in the creation of the State of Israel, the unequal division of land between Arabs and Jews, and the separation of the Armenian community living on the Israeli side from those on the Arab side, particularly in the Old City of Jerusalem and the Armenian Quarter.

In Jerusalem the fighting was more intense and protracted in 1948 than in Jaffa or Haifa and the Armenian Patriarchate of Jerusalem and the Armenian Quarter were dragged into the violence. The most severe attacks between Arabs and Jews took place to the east by Zion Gate where the Armenian and Jewish Quarters lay side by side. To a lesser extent, there was fighting down the incline around the homes of my grandparents, and the Nammari and Weingarten families in the direction of the Jewish Quarter.

On August 2, 1948, during an intense siege of the Old City of Jerusalem with substantial destruction that included monasteries and church institutions, a delegation of the Greek, Catholic, and Armenian churches visited Count Bernadotte at Augusta Victoria on the Mount of Olives seeking protection for holy sites and the ending of hostilities in Jerusalem.[111]

The Armenian *Kaghakatsis* had stayed in their homes outside the Armenian Convent throughout earlier sporadic violence in 1947, but some moved to the Convent for safety in December 1947 and were accommodated in the school, which was the only space available. Other *Kaghakatsis* waited until early May before they took refuge in the Convent or in the Christian Quarter. They were later moved to the St James Cathedral. A protection committee was established at the Patriarchate to organize and manage the crisis, and attempts were made to guard deserted houses in the Armenian Quarter.

Armenians fleeing violence or who lost their property in what became Israel took refuge in the Armenian Convent *(Vank)*, which was once again obliged to accommodate hundreds of refugees in already crowded premises. Less than 30 years earlier, the Patriarchate had struggled to accommodate survivors of the Genocide. Now refugees had to be accommodated in cellars and stables in underground passages which had not been used for decades. Conditions were stuffy, dark, dirty, and there were fears of epidemic due to limited water supplies. Sir Henry Gurney

An excerpt from Sir Henry Gurney's[112] diary reflects the standing of Patriarch Guregh Israelian, the respect people held him in, and his wisdom. Knowing that the Mandate was ending, Sir Henry took time to bid farewell to the Patriarch a day before he left Palestine. The disaster that befell the refugees, and the burden of meeting needs as Armenians turned to the Patriarchate for food and shelter, was a matter of the utmost concern and was referred to by Sir Henry in this short note.

> *"A farewell visit to the Armenian Patriarchate 13th*
> *May 1948*
> *Yesterday I called on the Armenian Patriarch, one*
> *of our best friends, and had a long talk with him in*
> *which he deplored our going. We sat at one of his*
> *vast green reception rooms crowded with portraits*
> *of former Patriarchs and Kings and Queens of*
> *England and discussed Jerusalem. How illogical it*
> *was, he said, to fight for a city because it is sacred*
> *and destroy it in so doing. If it were really looked*

*upon as so sacred as people said, they would not
fight and murder in its streets and so kill its sanctity.
The truth was that Jerusalem was and had always
been the political and strategic key: the only Arab
north –south road in Palestine passed through it
entering Allenby Square; the only remaining road
from the east into central Palestine passed through
it from Allenby Bridge, the ancient road from
Philadelphia (Amman) to Jaffa. As the Kawasses
with their tapping sticks conducted me out down
the long stone corridor, I looked back and saw him
for the last time, waiving faintly at the top of the
steps about to return to the problems of handling his
2,000 refugees and keeping peace for his community
in the Old City, crowded as they were into a corner
between Arab and Jews. "*[113]

Contributions from wealthier local Armenians to the Patriarchate
dwindled when most of these families lost their businesses,
property, and livelihoods; some became recipients of aid rather
than benefactors. This was coupled with mounting challenges in
responding to the daily needs of Armenians in the Convent, in the
Armenian Quarter, and beyond in the Holy Land with increasing
unemployment and poverty.

Several properties owned by the Armenian Patriarchate of Jerusalem
were located in an area that became Israel and were no longer
easily accessible by the Armenian Patriarchate located on the Arab
side. Jaffa, Bethlehem and Jerusalem were three key cities where
Armenian religious and cultural life was lost and became inaccessible.
Ties with Armenians who stayed in what became the State of Israel
were severed and families with members in both areas were separated
from each other.

Following the partition of Palestine, the Armenian Church in what became Israel was faced with Israeli laws on marriage according to the rabbinical court rather than state laws. Marriage between a Jew and a non-Jew was not legal, and the Church was unable to serve those with interfaith relationships. Similarly, any conversion from Judaism to Christianity was problematic and those responsible for the conversion could be accused of proselytization.[114]

The Patriarchate also faced the challenge of repairing property destroyed in the Armenian Quarter. Lack of free access to the property and holy sites now under Israeli control prompted appeals to the international community. On April 30, 1948, Patriarch Guregh Israelian joined the Custos of the Holy Land P. Alberto Gori and Archbishop Athenagoras, Ecumenical Patriarch (1948–1972) for the Greek Orthodox Patriarch of Jerusalem, as heads of the Christians and Guardians of the Holy Places in signing a letter requesting the High Commissioner for Palestine to transmit the following message to his Majesty's Government in London and the United Nations Organization:

"Perturbed by the present situation in Palestine and basing our request on incidents which have already occurred necessitating the withdrawal of our Ecclesiastical guardians and priests from our Institutions and Religious Establishments in Tiberias and Haifa: and the fighting today around the Orthodox Monastery and Church of St. Simeon in Katamon, Jerusalem, we emphasize our fears as to the security and respect of sanctity of the Shrines and Places sacred to all Christians of the world regardless of confession. We appeal to those organizations now deliberating on the future and security of the Holy Land to take very urgent and immediate action to ensure the safety and security

> *of all Christian Sanctuaries in Jerusalem and*
> *throughout Palestine. Further we request, that*
> *definite steps be taken immediately to ensure that on*
> *the termination of the British Mandate there shall*
> *exist an authority capable of ensuring the practical*
> *administration and good government of Jerusalem*
> *and its environs including Bethlehem, Mt. of Olives,*
> *and Ain Karem.* "[115]

The Armenian Patriarchate of Jerusalem faced another challenge, namely the election of a new Patriarch when Israelian passed away in October 1949.[116] The Armenian Apostolic See of St. James remained vacant for a long time with internal strife between Archbishops Yeghishe Derderian and Tiran Nersoyan which culminated in the election of Derderian as the 95th Patriarch of Jerusalem (1960). The struggle between the two claimants for the position of Patriarch was finally resolved with US intervention (which was concerned about Nersoyan's potential sympathy with communism). Jordanian laws and courts governed procedures for the selection of religious leaders but internal strife about the patriarchal seat was heated hed within a community that was divided in its support for the candidates.[117] Community tensions continued for some time.

The respect and love people had for Patriarch Israelian was reflected in the following uttered in various interviews :

> *" I marched with the scouts during Israelian's funeral*
> *which was attended by a large crowd weeping his*
> *loss.* "[118]

> *"Israelian was a strong man and true leader*
> *committed to the welfare of his people. He was*
> *always around his people trying to calm them and*
> *attend to their needs. He opened the Patriarchate*

*with every vacant corner to accommodate the
terrified and helpless refugees. He was a great loss
to the Patriarchate and the community."[119]*

The leadership of Patriarch Israelian is evident in his engagement in
the Brotherhood, and with his community and beyond. The words
of sympathy uttered by diplomats, church leaders, and others reflect
what this theologian believed and stood for

*"Noble and great man with high standing and
great qualities.....with whom we worked with
great cordiality and mutual respect....a profound
theologian.....a generous benefactor to those in
need....a true man in face of physical danger.....a
friend of other churches ....a pious leader who did
much for his community and others ....a truly loyal
counsellor and friend whose life was lived solely to
serve others ...radiance coming from him not failing
to affect those around him."[120]*

The Christ Church centre (which accommodated Palestinian Arabs
and Armenians during the 1948 War) comprises a church, hostel,
parsonage, school hall, and classrooms. It adjoins the Citadel which,
together with Jaffa Gate, forms a fortress at the southwest corner of
the City wall and commands one of the two road entrances into the
Old City. The Armenian Patriarchate of Jerusalem (accommodating
Armenians) and Christ Church were the main sites in the Old City
for the internally displaced in 1948. Both are located a short distance
inside Jaffa Gate. Both were also close to the Jewish neighborhood of
Montefiore just outside the walls of the Old City, from which several
attacks were launched on Jaffa Gate and the Citadel to break through
to relieve the Jewish Quarter in the Old City, which lies immediately
behind Christ Church and the Armenian Quarter. Thus, the whole
Jaffa Gate area and all the way to the Armenian Quarter lay in the

line of both Arab and Jewish fire. Rev. Hugh Jones (rector from 1945-1964), stated in his diary:

> *"The Armenian Patriarch collecting his flock living in the Armenian Quarter and brought them inside the Convent walls, where 3,000-4,000 Armenians were collected, many of them living in tents erected in the grounds. On May 18th a building in the Armenian Compound was struck by a heavy shell and partly demolished, causing several casualties in killed and wounded. One Armenian came over and begged me to get in touch by phone (none of their phones were working) with a Red Cross delegate and ask if representations could be made to Jews and Arabs to avoid shelling the crowded Armenian Compound.......*

> *"I visited the Armenian Patriarch on May 25th, the explosions of the previous night were shells falling on the Armenian Compound. Two struck the Cathedral, one demolished a small house, wounding the dozen occupants and bringing total casualties to date to 130 including seven dead. Considerable damage has been caused by shells, which have driven the 3,000-4,000 people into underground caves. The condition under which these people are living beggars description. Crowded into stuffy, airless, underground passages; filling the churches to overflowing, short of water, fearing epidemics, their future is black indeed unless a big change in the situation takes place, or unless at least 1,000 or more can be removed to some safer place to relieve the congestion."*[121]

Reverend Jones described the dramatic conditions of refugees packed into the Armenian Convent. Despite the challenges, the Armenian Patriarchate of Jerusalem was fully committed to attending to the needs of Armenians and non-Armenians seeking assistance from the Patriarchate. It provided meals to Armenians and some non-Armenians[122] who approached the Convent and attended to the needs of the injured to ease people's misery. There are no descriptions about how the religious space turned into a refugee camp and there is a paucity of stories documenting daily life in the Convent during that period.

Patriarch Guregh Israelian, who served as Armenian Patriarch of Jerusalem from 1944 to 1949, gathered around him the members of the Brotherhood and shouldered responsibility for the welfare of Armenians spiritually and materially. In January 1948, after the Armenian Christmas celebrations and with increasing conflict and threat of violence between Arabs and Jews, the Armenian fund committee for the needy collected 1,000 Palestinian pounds from members of the community.[123]

Israelian is remembered for his genuine care for his flock. He would move through the Convent and from one home to another checking on people and their needs, and seeking every penny for the benefit of his people. Hintlian's father had worked at the Patriarchate as secretary and aide to the Patriarch, and had been very fond of Israelian who he dealt with on a daily basis. One cold winter evening in 1948, he spotted Israelian sitting alone around a non-lit brazier wearing two coats. When he asked Israelian why there was no fire lit, Israelian responded that he needed to economize and save whatever he could for his people. This tells us much about the character of Israelian and why he is remembered as a caring and kind Patriarch who always attended to the needs of his Church and followers.

Patriarch Guregh Israelian. Photo provided by Kevork Hintlian.

Within the walls of the Armenian Convent, Armenians organised three groups: one responsible for health care, a second to deal with food provisions and water distribution, and a third group to protect the Armenian Quarter from shelling by the *Haganah*. These groups were formed under the directive of Patriarch Israelian. Both *Kaghakatsis* and *Vanketsis* formed a civil guard to defend the Armenian Quarter from the two warring parties. Armenian civil guards armed with makeshift weapons united with priests of the Brotherhood of St. James under the leadership of two priests.

The Patriarch set up an emergency steering committee that included an executive committee, relief committee, disciplinary committee, and a health committee. These were prepared for the disaster in 1948 and catered to the emerging needs created by the fighting and the influx of Armenian families into both St. James and the Bethlehem Armenian monastery.

Սուրբ Սակոբ Վանք, Գարտիզպատ, 1948-ին Արաբ-Իսրայէլեան Պատերազմի ժամանակ, Հայ հսկիչ պահակներ:

Armenian civil guards patrolling Bardizatagh during the 1948 Arab-Israeli war, take time out to mug for the photographer.
(Photo courtesy Mr Antranig Bakerjian)

Armed Armenians in the Armenian Convent in 1948. Photo provided by Saro Nakashian. The man standing on the right wearing a kufiyyeh wa iqal (male headdress) is probably an Arab.

A soup kitchen opened at the Armenian Convent to serve all Armenians in 1948 and for 10 years afterwards. Armenians who had lost everything - some for the second time - and who had become destitute made use of what was offered through the kitchen, in which over fifteen employees attended to storage areas, received foodstuffs provided by UNRWA, and cooked and served food. The kitchen served up to seven hundred meals a day and up to 250,000 meals a month. This was a huge undertaking for an organisation which in a short time had to attend to needs at least 20 times more than its traditional capacity. The strain on its infrastructure was enormous. To most of the community however, this kitchen was their lifeline during tough times.[124]

"The kitchen would sometimes provide children with custard and muhalabiyyeh (milk and cornflour desert) in addition to the meals. This was our treat and a source of joy and happiness as we found ourselves in crowded dwellings after the destruction of our home and with little income. Thankfully, there was the kitchen and an entity that embraced us in our suffering by giving us shelter and food."[125] Women helped the main chefs (the Jambazian brothers) in preparing the food, and several men and women volunteered to help on a daily base.[126]

Սուրբ Ճակոբ Վանք, Պարտիզպարագ. 1948-ին Արաբ-Իսրայելեան Պատերազմի ընթացքին; զատրակեան Հայ ժողովուրդին կերակուր հայթայթելու համար շինուած փուռը սեղանատան վերածուած։
   Little children line up for their daily gruel served in the bakery-turned-kitchen of Bardizatagh during the 1948 Arab- Israeli war.
   (Photo courtesy Mr Antranig Bakerjian)

> *"For the few lucky children whose family could give them some money to spend, Murad Zadoyan's canteen in the Keeraj Khana basement in the Convent was the place to buy sweets, albeit with very limited options. Other children were unable to buy sweets for a long time until the opportunity appeared during Armenian Christmas in January 1949, when the Homenetmen women distributed sweets to children in the Convent."[127]*

My mother Lucy Khatcherian, who was almost 13 years old at that time, stated:[128]

> *"With the increasing violence, it was hard for my family of nine to stay outside the Convent near Souk El Hussor in the Old City. We took shelter in the Convent and left everything behind, unaware that we would never return to that residence again. We were given a shared space with other families in the Convent.*

> *"We had no clothes except for those we had on when we left our home, and we stayed in the same clothes for over two weeks. I think they were washed once while most of us children were left naked until our clothes dried. The first time we changed our clothes is when we arrived in Al Salt[129] and were offered clothing by my aunt who was married there. Through her husband, we were transported to Al Salt. We took no baths for days. It made us appreciate more the opportunities we had when bathing in the hamam (public Turkish baths) in the Old City. Not only was there enough hot water but it was an opportunity to mingle with others and socialize.*

"Our food was provided by the kitchen in the Convent. We had no money or means to buy food. We had to be content with whatever we were offered, and we were thankful to eat. The food was simple but even a few bites were satisfying. Young men at the Vank used to bring us food once a day and we would divide it among us. Sometimes an additional piece of bread with cheese would be distributed at another time of the day, but not always. Small pieces divided by nine would end up as a bite or two....it was not much but it somehow filled our stomachs.

"We would hear the bombing and were scared, especially when it intensified at night. We stayed indoors most of the time - day and night. The time when we would be outside is when we lined up to use the shared latrines early in the morning or to get food in a long queue. Latrine conditions were horrible to say the least. Again, we were thankful. You refer to crowding and yes, the Convent was packed with people everywhere in every available space. Also, I remember taking shelter in the church at times where you would not see an inch of empty space. It was filled with women, children, and men of all ages as one huge family. We resorted to prayer a lot and were very saddened by the news of those killed or wounded. There was a great sense of solidarity. We were all affected by what was going on around us, very fearful of the unknown and wondered when it would all be over."

Photo of Lucy's family.From family archive with Lucy on the left standing next to her mother (early 1940s).Two sisters born between 1946 and 1948 are missing from the Photo.

My mother often spoke of this experience with bitterness and with tears flowing from her eyes. She used to connect her family's experience in 1948 with what she and her siblings heard from her parents on their ordeal as orphaned refugees fleeing their village (Everek) in Ottoman Turkey. She would repeat what my grandmother used to often say in Armenian, *Mekhk Hayere Lav Ormeh Chidesan* (Poor Armenians, have never seen a good day). For my mother, 1948 was a disaster but it paved the way for her future career as a nurse at 15 years of age when she assisted nurses at a medical center in Al Salt, where her family settled after 1948, before she joined the Augusta Victoria Hospital nursing program in Jerusalem in 1953 and moved steadily in her career.

Berj Gegekoushian described 1948 as catastrophic for Armenians:

> *"The Jerusalem Armenian community was in shock
> and bombarded with hundreds of refugee Armenians.
> We depended greatly on the Patriarchate for
> our sustenance. It was the bread, burghul, rice,
> macaroni, white beans, and lentils offered to us by
> the Patriarchate that kept us alive. There was no
> meat, fruit or vegetables. Food was running out
> quickly in 1948.*

> *"I vividly remember Patriarch Israelian, who was
> caring and committed to his people, speaking to the
> Armenian community: 'My dear Armenians, I have
> appealed to rich Armenians in the diaspora to come
> to your rescue and aid but in vain. I have sent a
> second appeal and still in vain. In my third appeal
> I said the Armenians here are frying without oil.
> Assistance eventually poured in.' As a result, each
> family received five pounds and trucks filled with
> assistance parked at the front of the main western
> gate of the Convent gave families fish, raisins, and
> walnuts, from which we ate for three months."*[130]

> *Relief services at the Convent were directed by
> Dr. Krikor Daghlian. The medical team comprised
> Krikor Daghlian, Puzant Semerdjian, Vartouhi
> Mardirossian and Khatoun Sarkissian, aided by
> Armenians trained in first aid who received the
> wounded in the newly equipped Convent infirmary.
> Stretchers carrying the wounded were occasionally
> rushed from the Convent to the hospital set up in the
> Austrian Hospice.*[131] *Daghlian and his team treated
> all wounded Armenians and 65 non-Armenians.*[132]

Fish, raisins, walnuts

1948ի Արաբ-Իսրայելեան պատերազմի օրերին, Միութեանս Կարմիր Խաչի անդամները։ Ա. շարք՝ ձախին աջ.-Գրիգոր Սարգիսեան, Սուրեն Ազգեան եւ Հաճն Սիմոնեան։ Բ. շարք՝ Շուշան Յովսէփեան, խաթուն Սարգիսեան, Տրր. Գրիգոր Տաղեան, Տրր. Բիւզանդ Մեմիրճեան, Վարդուհի Մատիրոսեան եւ Յակոբ Մէնշեան։ Գ. շարք՝ Ճօն Պապասեան, Shգրան Պետրոսեան, Կարապիս Օհանեան, Կարապետ Շահխասարեան, Յակոբ Համոյեան, Յովսէփ Անտոնեան, Ղազարոս Քիշմիշեան եւ Հեղում Պետիկեան։ Դ. շարք՝ Արամ Մկրտիչեան, Պօղոս Էմէրզեան, Սարգիս Աբիբեան, Գրիգոր Թխչունձեան, Լեւոն Տաղեան, Սարօ Նազիկեան եւ Գէորգ Յովսէփեան։

The Armenian writing under the photo reads: 1948 Arab Israeli war days.
Armenian Red Cross members.[133]

The infirmary and the medical team were housed in the basement of the St Thoros Church, which was converted into a makeshift hospital. The medical team at the Armenian infirmary worked around the clock and cared for all first aid and minor surgery needs. The assistants of the infirmary medical team were graduates of the Armenian school and young men from the Young Men's Society who were trained to offer first aid. Their reputation spread throughout the Old City as they had treated cases where hidden pieces of shrapnel were detected and extracted in the infirmary even after the wounded had undergone surgery in the hospital. Thus, their work was held in high regard by hospital surgeons. Delegates from the Holy See of Lebanon visited the infirmary in the first week of June 1948 and brought with them funds raised by the Armenian General Benevolent Union (AGBU). Dr.

Krikorian came to work in the infirmary and join the medical team. Another batch of medications was sent by Armenian pharmacists from Cairo and Alexandria.[134]

The more established Armenian communities in Egypt and Lebanon, being a bit further from the battlefield, extended their arms to their brothers and sisters in the Holy Land. These same communities and their host countries received and assisted Armenians who left Palestine and took refuge there. The coordinated work under crisis and challenging times would not have been possible and effective without the rapid mobilization of groups internally through the efforts of Patriarch Israelian, the Brotherhood, and key people in the Armenian community, and externally by the Armenian diaspora through the long standing status of the Armenian Church abroad, and the connections of influential people in these host countries.

> *"The Austrian Hospice was turned into the main hospital in the Old City to which most injured in the Old City who needed hospital treatment and surgery were transported day and night. It was always over-occupied with the injured. There were three smaller hospitals/centers: Spafford for Children in the Muslim Quarter, the Hilal maternity center behind the Austrian Hospice, and the Eye Hospital near Souk El Hussor (the carpet market), but the injured were not sent to these hospitals, although the hospitals may have treated a few with minor injuries. The Augusta Victoria Hospital[135] (AVH) on the Mount of Olives was also used. Several Armenian nurses were already working in those centers in 1948. I remember that Dr. Ibrahim Tleel was well known and took care of the wounded. Also Dr Amin Majaj and his wife Betty who worked from*

Bethany. There were not many Arab physicians at that time, and not enough to meet the increasing casualties of war." [136]

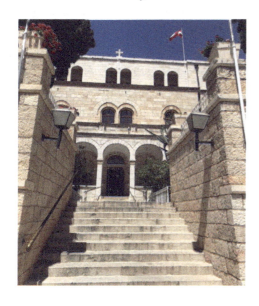

The entrance to the Austrian Hospice in the Old City of Jerusalem. Photo credit Sana'a Hasna, 2022.

A corridor in the Austrian Hospice once used as a hospital ward.[137] *Photo credit Sana'a Hasna, 2022.*

Varouj Ishkhanian was 16 years old in 1948 and lived next to the St. Mark's Syriac Church in the Old City, adjacent to the Armenian Quarter. His family of five (mother, two sisters and brother) moved with Varouj to the Armenian Convent in 1948. His father stayed in their house fearful of looting. Varouj stated:

> *"I remember carrying what we had in storage of flour, rice, sugar, and legumes. My mother prepared our food and was not ready to receive food distributed to all in the Convent. We were assigned a room. We ate either rice or burghul daily.*

> *"My memories of 1948 include many children in the Convent. Barracks were put up by the Red Cross (Garmeer Khatch) in the large garden and later moved to Keeraj Khana. More than 200 mortars fell on the Patriarchate. I remember Patriarch Israelian as a serious, rarely smiling, clergyman. All the rooms in the Convent were full with five to eight people in each room. The Convent gates were usually kept closed but the main entrance was opened sometimes to allow for passage.*

> *"The Convent was overcrowded and even the Echmiadzin Church (St James Cathedral) housed some 20 families separated by hung blankets. I remember several families who also took refuge inside the Convent, including Apraham Aghabekian (Studio London) from the Musrara, the Demirgians from Al Thory, Setrag Didizian from Baqa'a, Kevork and Stepan Hagopian, the Shohmelians, and others."*

Alongside the violence and war in 1948, there was an outbreak of smallpox that had started in Transjordan and reached Bethany. This required that the population be vaccinated. Through the efforts of Patriarch Israelian, vaccines were brought from Beirut and the entire Armenian community was vaccinated. This was followed by an outbreak of typhoid and diphtheria in Palestine.[138] The infirmary team had to deal with these problems as well as the difficulties facing relief efforts during a period of war. Medical supplies depleted rapidly but the Patriarchate managed to maintain incoming supplies albeit at minimal levels. The Armenian men and women volunteers continued with utmost commitment to contribute in whatever way possible to cater to the needs of a community in distress.[139]

Կարմիր Խաչի տղաքը՝ գործի պահուն։

Red Cross boys at work. Photo from the Hoyetchmen anniversary book.

Grave losses of businesses and property befell Armenians who fled to the Armenian Quarter from West Jerusalem and other cities in Palestine. Like the dispossessed and displaced Palestinians, they were under the impression and hope that they would soon return home. However, they quickly realized that their forced exile had become permanent. Of the Armenians who left to Jordan, some returned

Forced exile to the Armenian Quarter

after a while, but others continued their way to Damascus, Beirut or elsewhere.

My mother's family was transported to Al Salt, a town in Transjordan, where her aunt (Tamom) was married to a Jordanian from the Hattar family. Tamom was a 13-year-old Genocide survivor who was lost in the desert on her march to Syria with her father (my great grandfather) and her brother (my maternal grandfather), her two remaining family members to survive from a family of eight. My grandfather had lost his mother, two brothers, and two of his three sisters. Tamom ended up in an orphanage in Syria and later, in an orphanage in Jordan, where she was adopted by a Jordanian Christian family(Hattar) who raised her as their child and had her marry one of their sons. She was reunited with her father and her brother (my grandfather) in the early 1930s after my great grandfather and grandfather arrived as pilgrims in Jerusalem and searched the archives of convents and orphanages for a lost green-eyed, fair-haired daughter. They finally found a note at the Armenian Convent in Jerusalem requesting any living relative of a young Armenian women named Tamom, with a description that matched their relative, to check with the elders of the town of Al Salt. Following this family reunion, my great-grandfather, grandparents and their three children moved to Al Salt in the early 1930s, then to Amman for a couple of years, and from there to Jerusalem in 1935. In 1948, Tamom's husband came in a truck and picked my mother's family from the Armenian Convent. They stayed in Al Salt and later in Amman for several years before emigrating to Lebanon, and from there to Jerusalem in the mid-sixties, and onwards to the US after the 1967 War. My grandparents and their descendants were continually on the move, twice refugees, and moving from one country to another with no sense of stability.

My aunt Vartoug was 18 in 1948 and she told me on several occasions about the uncertainties they experienced, especially moving to Al

Salt and Amman:

> *"You can imagine what goes through your head when you have left your home in haste and fear. It was one thing moving to the Convent for safety, but another moving to the Jordanian side and leaving everything behind, not knowing where we were going, where we would stay, what we would do. How would we move on with no work and income? Would we come back? What would our new life be like? Will we be able to manage? What about our neighbors who were our larger family?*

> *"We did not have relatives at all as my parents were orphaned during the Armenian Genocide, but they had very close friends considered like family. Hagop Ramian (Abu Yousef), also a Genocide survivor, was one such friend with whom my father had worked in construction and we were close family friends. Im Simon was also a good friend and neighbor. Would our paths meet again?*

> *"The questions were numerous with no answers and our anxiety was mounting. We were calmed by our parents' assurances that they had seen worse days and that this too would pass. The most important thing was that we were together and alive even though we were homeless and penniless. I often wondered how much more Armenians should have to endure. Despite my parents' assurances, I was always worried - how can they endure all of this, what gives them all this strength to stay put. They still reminisced about the atrocities of the Genocide, which I was sure they had not or ever could forget.*

They were already living an extended trauma and now this, an additional trauma. With time, I realized that it was their belief and faith that kept them safe and helped them to move on. This was something we as a family learned from them."[140]

Armenians fleeing in 1948 from Palestine to Syria, Jordan, Lebanon and Cyprus created a second community of Armenians in those countries of refuge. Armenian Palestinian refugees joined Armenian communities already living in these countries, having found refuge there in the early 19th century in the aftermath of the Armenian Genocide. Armenians were established in those countries of refuge and the dynamics between the earlier community and the new refugees because of the *Nakba* resembled that of the *Kaghakatsi* and the *Zuwwar* in the Holy Land in the aftermath of the Genocide. Furthermore, the accommodation of Armenian refugees of 1948 in host countries and communities was for whole families (like my maternal grandparents and their children) and not for orphans (as both my maternal grandparents had been).

Despite their misery, my mother, aunts and uncle counted their blessings compared to what they had heard from their parents about being orphaned refugees with no sense of family after the slaughter of their relatives during the Armenian Genocide. The sense of togetherness was of utmost importance and a means of coping. I have always wondered how they stayed close even though they ended up years later in different parts of the world. My aunt Vartouhi would always say: *"We made it, we worked hard in Jordan, in Lebanon, in Jerusalem and the US, and we looked after each other .There was no way we would go through or endure a repeat of the past."*

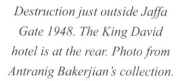

Destruction just outside Jaffa Gate 1948. The King David hotel is at the rear. Photo from Antranig Bakerjian's collection.

The Shelling of the Armenian Quarter

The 28 acres of the Armenian Quarter (one-sixth of the Old City), which developed into an Armenian enclave and dominated Armenian life in the Holy Land, underwent shelling and destruction in 1948 from the *Haganah,* and from crossfire between Jewish and Arab fighters. No area of the Armenian cemetery on Mount Zion and the St. Saviour

Armenian convent within the cemetery's compound was spared. The cemetery's location just outside Zion Gate was very strategic as it was one of the main sites where Jewish militias were located by Dormition Abbey and from where fire was exchanged with Arab soldiers inside the wall.

The entrance to the Armenian cemetery on Mount Zion. To the rear is the dome of the Dormition Abbey. Photo by author.

The Armenian cemetery was subjected to heavy shelling and many graves were partially or fully destroyed. Some soldiers hid in the graves by removing the top and stepping inside. When the war ended, the cemetery was in "no man's land" outside the walls of the Old City and became inaccessible to Armenians in East Jerusalem, which fell under Jordanian rule. In December 1948, and availing of the truce, the real estate department at the Armenian Patriarchate verified the condition of the St. Savior Monastery on Mount Zion from the walls of the Old City. It was in a half-ruined condition.[141]

Destruction at the Armenian cemetery on Mount Zion. Photo from Antranig Bakerjian's collection.

Looters desecrated graves and opened the graves of Patriarchs hoping to find items of value. Several other tombs were ruined.

Grave of a Patriarch at the Armenian cemetery on Mount Zion with a chipped top (center-right) and bullet marks on the front. Photo by author.

One source summarized the situation of the Patriarchate in 1948: *The Armenian Orthodox Patriarchate was hit by about one hundred mortar bombs thrown by Zionists from the Monastery of the Benedictine Fathers on Mount Zion. The bombs damaged St. Jacob's Convent, the Archangels Convent and their two Churches, their two elementary and seminary schools, and their library. Eight people among the refugees were killed and 120 wounded.*[142]

The Armenian Convent also bore its share of shelling from the communication trenches in the cemetery and was hard hit in 1948. Several bombs fell on St. James Street over a number of days. Some bombs fell on the gardens of the Patriarchate, on the seminary building, in the courtyard of the quarter for new priests, in the old priests' quarter in the forecourt of St. James Cathedral, on the roof of St. Echmiadzin near the belfry, in residential quarters, on the Kalaydjian wheat factory, in front of the Gulbenkian library, on St. Saviour's at the *Pergeetch,* and on the roof of the Convent. Jirair Tutunjian stated:

> *"My first memory is the roar of mortars as they fell on the Armenian Convent. I was two-and-a-half years old and hiding under the blanket in my parents' bed. When the mortar crashed into the yard of a neighbor's home, barely forty yards away, our home shook and dust from the ceiling rained on me and on the blanket. I hid my head deeper into the blanket."*[143]

Shelling destroyed shops, pavements, rooms, and there was considerable material damage and human loss. Overall, some 40 Armenians died and more than 400 were wounded in the brief War of 1948.

Notes in the May-June 1948 *Sion* magazine referred to:

> *"Continuation of Jewish bombing of the Old City during 23-25 May ....electricity and lighting cables*

are broken due to the bombings .....The government water supply has stopped. On May 20th a huge bomb exploded on the rooftop of the Holy Etchmiadzin Church in the convent which caused great damage to the bell tower and the rooftop..... Bombs have exploded near the Grand Sacristan's house and other neighborhoods in the convent .....

King Abdullah I visited the Church of the Holy Sepulcher on May 27th wearing military uniform and was welcomed by the Armenian and Greek Patriarchs and the Custos of the Holy Land ...... On May 28th the Jewish Quarter falls to the hands of the Jordanian army....from May 29th to 31st the shelling on the Old City was reduced and it was easier to move from place to place in the city. Following the opening of the roads to Amman, Armenians left Jerusalem to Amman or Beirut due to the situation....."

The *Sion* editorial of July- August 1948 stated:

"It was heartbreaking seeing the Brotherhood and the community standing together to go through this difficulty.....the tragedy has now ended. The Palestinian horizon will stay gloomy and red (metaphor)....The Holy See (Patriarchate) is facing tremendous difficulty. The Palestinian tragedy deprived the Patriarchate of its real estate and income....We seek help from Armenians in the diaspora'.

On June 10, 1948, Patriarch Guregh sent the following message to the Security Council of the United Nations:

"....since the 15th of May 1848, the Basilica of the Holy Sepulcher of Jesus Christ and other Holy Places within the Walls of the Old City of Jerusalem and its environs, as well as cathedrals, churches, monasteries, convents, educational and charitable institutions within the same area, have been bombarded with mortar shells and riddled with bullets and grenades, seriously damaging several of them .We therefore appeal to you most earnestly to take urgent steps which would ensure the protection and safety of the Holy Places and sacred Institutions in Jerusalem and throughout Palestine."[144]

The children and grandchildren of those who lived the experience of 1948 in the Armenian Quarter commonly claim that St. James protected Armenians in the Convent and in the Armenia Quarter from harm. It is believed that a mysterious figure dressed in white, which people identified as St. James, stood on the dome of St James monastery to protect those in the Church and that he diverted mortars with his hands.[145]

"As fighting intensified and it was not safe to stay in the Armenian Quarter, my grandmother Almaza took my mom Nevart and my Aunt Mary Kukeyan to the Armenian Convent. They were given a room where the priests' dorms are located today. They stayed there for six months in a small 3x4 room along with two of the Alemian sisters who were living in West Jerusalem and who came to the Convent for safety. They were five or six people in the room with no money.

"Once the truce was signed, they went back to find the house empty. My grandmother decided to go to Beirut where her daughter Martha was married to the Arab Armouny family. She sought transport with the Petra taxis which used to line up at Jaffa Gate. She was penniless but had a gold earring which she promised to give to the driver upon arrival to Beirut. It was a very long day and the two young ladies (Nevart 19 and Aida 7) became very hungry. With no money, no food could be purchased. On the way, the driver picked up a young man who turned out to be Armenian. Noticing the ladies were hungry, he asked the driver to stop at Shtoura and bought lebaneh (sour cream) sandwiches for my grandmother, Nevart and Aida. Both Aida and Nevart were very happy to eat the sandwiches, but grandmother refused to eat."

"My grandmother and mother often used to speak of this experience with pain. Before 1948, the family had run two cafes behind Barclays Bank near Jaffa Gate and now they had become impoverished waiting for help from others."[146]

Although he was only three years old in 1948, Hintlian said that one of the few things he remembers from his early childhood is a powerful bomb blast that shattered windows and walls opposite St. James Cathedral and tore off the whole corner. Years later, this was confirmed by Hintilian's grandmother and mother who described how the blast filled their home with white and black dust while the grandmother hugged the boy to protect him with her body.

"When I was older, I learned from my father, among other things, that it was this blast that prompted him to take his family elsewhere. Apart from my father who stayed in Jerusalem, our family left to Beirut through Ramleh, stayed in Beirut for a short time, then travelled to Cyprus by sea and stayed with relatives in Larnaca. Our stay there spanned three years after which we returned to Jerusalem."[147]

Սուրբ Յակոբ Վանք, Գաղթականաց 1948-ին Արաբ-Իսրայելեան Պատերազմի ժամանակ ապաստան գաղթական Գարտիզաղաց ժողովուրդին:
Armenian refugees find shelter behind sandbags at Bardizatagh during the 1948 Arab-Israeli war.
(Photo courtesy Mr Antranig Bakerjian)

Bomb blast damage to the staircase in the main courtyard (Mendz Bardez) at the Convent 1948. Photo from Antranig Bakerjian's collection.

An account of the shelling is presented in Annex 1 and covers entries from then Father Yeghishe Derderian's diary. His descriptions shed light on the gravity of events in 1948 and its impact on Armenians and the Armenian Quarter.

On the night of July 16, 1948, over 500 shells were fired during seven hours of continuous shelling from the Jewish side of the city. In the Armenian Quarter, large mortars penetrated roofs, destroyed windows and doors, and damaged water tanks and walls. It was a night of horror with mortars falling constantly.[148]

The night of September 12 was the climax of suffering and a day of mourning for Jerusalem Armenians. Six coffins moved into the St. James Cathedral and were placed in front of the altar. The St. James Cathedral shook with the sobs of relatives and the congregation in the presence of the entire Brotherhood and the Patriarch. All of Jerusalem was in shock and the commander of the Transjordan forces, the heads of Christian churches, and prominent Jerusalem figures expressed condolences to the Patriarch and the community.[149]

Key dates and events referred to in Yeghishe's diary included May 27 and 28, and November 1948. His entries reflect the fear and suffering that dominated Armenian families stuck between survival and the ongoing turbulence.

- Although the Armenian *Kaghakatsis* stayed in their homes outside the Convent in the Armenian Quarter throughout the intermittent fighting and violence prior to 1948, they had to move to the Convent for safety reasons in December 1947 and were accommodated in the school, which was the only space available by then. A protection committee was established to guard deserted houses in the Quarter.

- The first serious signal of impending fighting was on the eve of May 14 with the demise of the British Mandate, the British abandoning their positions in Jerusalem, and the Arab and Jewish fighters trying to occupy those vacant positions. There were three vacant positions on the borders of the Jewish and Armenian Quarters. This invariably brought the Armenian Quarter into the line of battle.

- On May 18, 1948, Transjordan forces occupied the Old City of Jerusalem and some neighborhoods outside the wall: from Jaffa Gate to Abu Thor and Mar Elias in the south and Damascus Gate, Musrara, Sheikh Jarrah and Mount Scopus to the north.

- On May 27, King Abdullah paid a visit to Jerusalem and visited the Mosque of Omar and the Holy Sepulcher. He was received with honors by the representatives of the three major Christian communities.

- On May 28, the fighters, religious leaders, and residents of the Jewish Quarter (2000) surrendered to Abdallah Al Tal, commander of the Jordanian forces. Abdallah Al Tal had appealed for surrender for three nights through loudspeakers. Subsequent negotiations took place in the Armenian school inside the Convent. Jewish men, women and children were handed to the Jewish military authorities outside Zion Gate, while the sick and the wounded were treated in the halls of the Armenian school and handed over the next day. Yeghishe adds that, considering the situation, the whole operation was dealt with in a very honorable manner with much credit to the Jordanian military commander.

- In November 1948, King Abdullah visited Jerusalem and Bethlehem. He was received with great honors by

British abandoned their positions in 1948.

representatives of the Christian communities in the Church of Nativity.

- There were negotiations between the Arab and Jewish military to asphalt the road between Jerusalem and Bethlehem before Christmas. The Jews shelved the proposal while the Arab military authorities offered their military road for movement. The Latins made their entry to the Church of the Nativity on Christmas Eve from Beit Jala (a town north of Bethlehem) aided by Jordanian and Egyptian soldiers.

Abdallah Al Tal is seated in the middle next to Patriarch Israelian and alongside Arab soldiers and Armenian community members. Fr. Hairig Aslanian is seated in the front row while Fr. Haigaser Donnigian (dragoman) is in the center of the second row behind Abdallah Al Tal. Photo taken in June 1948 in the yard of the Church of the Holy Archangels (Hrishtagabed) in the Armenian Convent. Photo provided by George Hintlian.

Injuries and Loss of Life

It is not easy to find a complete list of the names of Armenians injured or killed. The list below was compiled from documents and interviews with relatives and friends to create the most inclusive account possible of the casualties of the deadly events. A list of those killed during the turbulent events leading to and during 1948 includes women, men and children, several of whom are buried inside the Convent in the *Keeraj Khanah*. The following is a non-exhaustive list:

In Jerusalem:
Women

- Eugenie Markarian, killed in the bombing of the King David.

- Anna Bedevian, 40 years old, killed by a casual bullet while she was hanging clothes outside her house located between the Armenian and Jewish Quarters.

- Anahit Ounjian, a young girl of eight years killed on May 25 by a bomb that fell in the main courtyard of the monastery.

- Anahid Poladian.

- Diamant Sahagian, 27 years old.

- Sirvart Seraydarian, aged 19, died on September 12 from wounds caused by a mortar that fell in the monastery courtyard.

- Lucine Seraydarian, aged 17, died on September 12 from wounds caused by a mortar that fell in a monastery courtyard.

Makrouhi Yeghissian, aged 20, was killed on September 12 from wounds caused by a mortar that fell in the monastery courtyard. Makrouhi and the Seraydarian sisters were killed while conversing under an archway. The Seraydarian mother, Srpouhy, went out in the dark to search for her daughters and was traumatized to find their disemboweled bodies. Yeghissian, Makrouhi's father was a diabetic and died a few days after his daughter Makrouhi was killed.[150]

Men

- Paraghamian, killed in the bombing of the King David.

- Sahag Sahagian, 30 years old, and his wife Diamant Sahagian, 27 years old, leaving behind a four-month-old daughter, Nevart Sahagian.

- Kevork Kevorkian, 15 years old, who died on May 18 from a bomb that fell on the new priests' quarters.

- Yesai Toumayan who died from the explosion of a bomb at Jaffa Gate.

- Haig Yanigian, 50 years old, from the explosion of a bomb at Jaffa Gate.

- Zakar Zakarian, 22 years old, on May 18 due to a bomb that fell in the forecourt of St. James Cathedral.

- Armen Hovsepian, 65 years old, on May 18 due to a bomb that fell in the forecourt of St. James Cathedral.

- Avedik Poladian, a 60-year-old lay monk was killed on May 18 by a bullet.

- Haroutoun Assadourian, 60 years old, on May 19 from wounds he sustained near the seminary.

- Paramaz Tel Ghazarian, 35 years old, killed on July 15 from an explosion of a bomb in the Greek Convent near the Holy Sepulchre.

- Haroutune Darghamian, 60 years old. His two daughters Sirvart and Lucine were to die on September 12.

- Manouk Seraydarian, 60 years old, the gate man of the monastery, killed on July 30 by a stray bullet.

- Hagop Matteosian, aged 21 was killed on Sept 12 by a mortar shell near the Lutheran Church.

- Karapet Dildilian, aged 25 was killed on Sept 12 by a mortar shell near the Lutheran Church.

- Boghos Aintablian, aged 40 was killed on Sept 12 by a mortar shell near the Lutheran Church.

- Ivan -Yervant Zakarian- aged 32 was shot by a sniper from the Notre Dame building across from New Gate and killed in 1948. He had three children under 10 years of age and his wife was pregnant with their fourth child.

In Haifa

- Noubar Momdjian
- Manuel Manougian, 38 years old
- Hagop Aintablian, 24 years old
- Three other young men.

In Jaffa

- Hovsep Shahinian, 26 years old
- Garabet Hagopian, 55 years old
- Kesabtsi Garabed, 25 years old
- Vahram Der Sahagian, 55 years old

Ivan (Yervant) Zakarian's son Michael recalled:

> *"I was five years old when my family and grandparents left in 1948 with our relatives, the Sultanians, to Amman because of the increased fighting. My mother was pregnant with my youngest sister. My father was called back to Jerusalem to*

work as he was an electrical engineer while we remained in Amman. One day while my father was walking back from work to the Armenian Quarter, passing between Al Zahra Gate and Damascus Gate, he was hit by a bullet from a sniper that caused a lot of bleeding. He was apparently taken to the Austrian Hospice in the Muslim Quarter.

"We were notified and immediately travelled back from Amman to Jerusalem. I remember we all went to the Hospice where my father was lying dead with his head bandaged. I still hear the weeping and sighs of my young, widowed mother who would await the birth of an already orphaned child. He was buried in the Convent cemetery; 1948 was a year of catastrophe for my family."[151]

Vartouhi Kukeyan stated that since childhood she had repeatedly been reminded of what had happened to her maternal uncle as an adolescent in 1948:

"My uncle Yesai Toumayan was a 16-year-old school student at the Terra Sancta School (West Jerusalem) when he was killed in June 1948 after a bomb has exploded in Jaffa Gate as he was coming back from school. He was an only brother among four sisters. He was rushed to the Hospice in the Old City but soon died from bleeding. On that day, my grandma had cooked a traditional Arab dish called makloubeh (upside down) which she never made again or ate thereafter.

"Yesai's death was a very traumatic event in the family and one which my mother and grandmother spoke

of with sorrow and pain. After this, my grandmother Almaza only wore black or brown. Yesai was buried very hastily in the Armenian cemetery on Mount Zion which was subject to crossfire between warring Jewish and Arab fighters. Only three people were present for the burial: my father who was 24 years old then and not yet married to my mother, our neighbor and my father's friend Hortanan Chillingirian, and a priest by the name of Haigaser. No one else could attend, not even Yesai's mother Almaza. He was the last Armenian to be buried in the cemetery before it became no man's land; it became accessible again after the 1967 Israeli occupation of the remaining parts of Palestine.

"After Yesai's burial, my grandmother frequently prayed that when she died, she would be buried next to her son. It was only after 1967 that my mother and grandmother could locate and visit Yesai's grave. When my grandmother passed away few years later, she was buried on top of him. Her wish came true and they both rest in peace."[152]

The grave of Almaza and her son Yesai Toumayan. Photo by author.

Several Armenians were injured around 1948. It is difficult to ascertain all the names and the following is a non-exhaustive list:

- Elisabeth Azizian, wounded in her arm by a bullet on May 15.

- 11 Armenians wounded on May 16 during a mass at St. James Cathedral when a large bomb and some smaller ones shook the Cathedral with the force of an earthquake.

- 32 wounded on May 18, some seriously, when a bomb fell in the courtyard of the new priest's quarter.

- 12 wounded in the evening of May 18 when a bomb fell in the forecourt of St. James Cathedral.

- Five wounded on May 19 from a bomb that fell in the large courtyard of the monastery.

- One youth wounded on May 19 when a shell exploded near the Holy Archangels Church.

- All members of the Ounjian family on the night of May 25 when three bombs fell in the main courtyard of the monastery.

- Five wounded on May 26 when bombs fell in the Patriarchate garden behind the library.

- Hrant Devedjian (a member of the Armenian Revolutionary Federation (ARF) defense squad) was wounded in the forehead on May 25.

- Eight wounded in the evening of May 27.

- Seven people (two women and five men) were wounded on July 10 when a bomb fell on the Convent roof and shrapnel caused injuries to those in the corridors underneath.

- Several wounded on July 16 by bombs that came through the roof.

- More than 27 were wounded on September 12 early in the morning by a mortar shell that landed at the main gate of the monastery while people were queuing for milk.

- Later in the day on September 12, four girls and women were wounded by a mortar which fell in a monastery courtyard.

The Heroes of the Time

The Armenian heroes of the time and the detailed events of 1948 remain part of the hidden unwritten stories barely covered in historiographies. Despite the fear, pain, destruction and suffering, several people rose to the call of duty and beyond in their efforts to safeguard the Armenian community at large. They defended the Armenian Quarter in 1948 while under a hail of bullets. Besides Patriarch Guregh Israelian, three clergymen stood out in 1948 as protectors of the Patriarchate:

1. Haigaser Donnigian was known as a courageous priest who conducted burial ceremonies for those killed despite the dangerous conditions of bombing and shooting. He also joined in digging graves. He was involved in the census in 1948 and went from house to house to obtain information.

2. Yeghisheh Derderian was the Grand Sacristan then and his political astuteness often safeguarded the Patriarchate.

3. Hairig Aslanian was the Chief Dragoman and a key person in the internal organization. Seven young Armenians reported daily on the news as they followed radio reports.[153]

The Patriarch ordered the establishment of three committees:[154]

1. An operations committee headed by the Patriarch with members Father Yeghishe Derderian, Bishop Souren

Kamhadjian, Fr. Norayr Bogharian, Krikor Daghlian, Nigoghos Chakmadjian, Sahag Sahagian, and Vartan Der Vartanian.

2.   A protection committee headed by Fr. Hairig Aslanian with members Hovannes Oungian, Sarkis Balian, Levon Stepanian, Simon Gulumerian, Kevork Kaplanian, Alexan Yaghiayan, Hrayr Yergatian, and Hagop Zakarian.

3.   A logistics committee headed by Father Meron Gerjigian with members Hovsep Shohmelian, Karnig Caloustian, Antranig Bakerjian, Apraham Toumayan, and Dajad Kasabian.

The three clubs around which the Armenian community's social and political life revolved divided up tasks to complement each other in safeguarding their community. [155]

1.   The *Hoyetchnmen* oversaw the work carried out by the Red Cross, cared for the wounded in the Convent infirmary, and transported those who needed advanced care to health centers outside the Convent.

2.   The *Homenetmen* were more involved in securing and using weapons for the defense of the Patriarchate and the community. Hintlian stated that two meetings were held: one civilian and one military. The former with with Rabbi Weingarten, the head of the Jewish community in the Jewish Quarter of the Old City, and the latter with the *Haganah*. Antranig Bakerjian had recently lost his aunt Bedevian in the shelling of their house but he rose above it all and brought Rabbi Weingarten to meet with Patriarch Israelian, who was trusted by the Jews of the Jewish Quarter for his neutrality. Despite this meeting, the shelling continued.

3.   Hrayr Yergatian is credited with arranging a second meeting in the Jewish Quarter, and for his attempts with a group of

eight armed Armenians, in a night at the height of shelling in May 1948, to showcase Armenian readiness to protect their community. Hintlian stated that this meeting projected an image of strength and of an Armenian community not to be overlooked. It was a clear message that the community was prepared. It was also a message to Arab fighters that Armenians were not taking sides but were ready to defend their Quarter with their lives.[156]

4. The *Parisiradz* had a dual role of field defense and medical relief. They also safeguarded Armenian homes in the Armenian Quarter outside the Convent.

The *Homenetmen* had been preparing arms for two years in anticipation of an eruption of violence. Some 70 Armenian men were armed, and this was one of the main reasons to take Armenians and the Armenian Quarter seriously. Guns were also purchased from disbanded British soldiers, while more Sten guns and weaponry became available after the fall of Gush Etzion. Armenian mechanic Keheyan is credited for training others on how to use the guns.[157] Elia/Yeghia Bedrossian, a blacksmith, was credited with making Italian-style guns for some of the men of the Armenian Quarter.[158] He was one of few Armenians who could diffuse mortars and saved many lives when he diffused unexploded bombs which landed in the Convent. He lost three fingers when dismantling one of these bombs.[159]

Heroes of the time from the *Kaghakatsi* community included[160] a group of 25 young men from the Armenian Quarter: Antranig Bakerjian, Hagop Zakarian (known as *Sab3 El Leil* - night wolf in Arabic), Robert Zakarian, Kevork Kukeyan (Kawarek), Apraham Toumayan, Murad Muradian, Garabed Hovsepian and Hortanan Chillingirian, Babigian, and others. They were responsible for bringing medical supplies, including bandages, antibiotics, and stretchers, from the

Austrian Hospice in the Muslim Quarter to the infirmary inside the Armenian Convent. They were also responsible for protecting abandoned homes in the Armenian Quarter from looting, collecting the dead for burial, and ensuring the injured received medical assistance. Bakerjian was the leader and the organizer.

> *"Hagop Zakarian was known as very courageous. He lived in the same courtyard where we lived in the Armenian Quarter with his mother, sister and brother Robert. He used to distribute food to people who didn't have much, and there were many in 1948. Antranig also did a lot in 1948. The Parisiradz was instrumental in helping the needy. My father Abcar Bannayan was the Kaghakatsi mukhtar and was aware of who needed what. Subsistence needs were mounting, and several families required food assistance. The Parisiradz did whatever it was able to do."*[161]

Those from the *Vank* included[162] Onnig Khacherian, Ghopukh Zaven, Antonig Dökmeji's (Deukmejian's) son, Furunji Avedis and his brother Kevork, Kevork Sevian, Hrant Devedjian, Shash Garbis Tavitian, Jeenjo Artin,[163] and "Kaassar"- Kassardjian's eldest brother who later emigrated to Uruguay. There was a dozen men or more. Jirair Tutunjian described his father working under difficult conditions:

> *"My father had been a telephone linesman and repairer of telephone lines during the Mandate. When war began in 1948 and Jordan took over East Jerusalem, my father was ordered (Arab Legion soldiers came to our house) to go out to repair broken telephone lines while bombs and bullets were still crisscrossing Jerusalem. He went out half-a-dozen times during the day and at night."*

My mother referred to Dakess as a young man from the Armenian Convent who went from door to door in and around the Armenian Quarter asking families to leave their house and gather in the Convent. He helped families to move to the Convent quickly as clashes were intensifying.[164] Pashayan and Nalbandian were responsible for securing drinking water, collecting refuse and organizing in general.

Vartouhi Kukeyan added:

> *"My father never said where they got guns from. They also had military attire. At one point, my paternal grandmother Vartoug threw the attire and the gun into the house well out of fear that they would be seen. This group of young and brave men tried to protect everyone's life, Armenians, Arabs and Jews alike. They were instrumental in accompanying the hundreds of Jewish men and women after the surrender of the Jewish Quarter on their march from the Jewish Quarter through the Armenian Convent, passing by the Armenian school inside the Convent, to Zion Gate ...in what had become the Jewishside."*[165]

Dikran Bakerjian recalled an incident proudly related to him by his father Antranig of a group of Jewish men who accessed the Armenian Quarter through the Convent gate facing Zion Gate in the Old City. They had passed through the Church of the Holy Archangels and from there, to the Armenian Quarter. They were stopped by Armenian men and a fist fight ensued next to the *Parisiradz* club. The intruders were released and pushed out through the same gate. There were no casualties but a strong instinct to protect the area. *"Antranig had a camera then and was known as the documentary person. Most of his film negatives and photos taken during 1948 were destroyed due to rain flooding a room where they were stored."*[166]

As a relatively small and politically neutral community positioned next to the Jewish Quarter, the Armenian community was not immune to accusations of siding with one or other of the warring parties. These accusations were disturbing and could have resulted in catastrophe. One day, Arab soldiers positioned on the city wall from the side of Zion Gate saw several men with weapons close to the Armenian museum area inside the Convent and thought that they were *Haganah* fighters who had managed to enter the Convent. Arab fighters marched towards the main Convent gate and tried to force their way in. The Armenians were fearful; the Patriarch preferred not to let anyone inside while Fathers Yeghishe and Hairig were in favor of letting the Arab fighters enter and see for themselves. Eventually, the Arab fighters were allowed in to find armed Armenians ready to defend and protect their lives, and the Convent protected by sandbags.[167] The lingering trauma of the Armenian Genocide, combined with the panic of the turbulent times, pushed Armenians to adopt measures to defend their Patriarchate, Convent, and Quarter as part of defending Jerusalem.

In another incident, four Armenians located in the *Hrishtagabed* area (the Church of the Holy Archangels) to safeguard the Convent from the east were caught by Arab fighters who accused them of helping Jewish fighters in the Jewish Quarter. They were later released unharmed through the intervention of Hagop Melikian[168] with Commander Abdallah Al Tal. Members of the Al Disi family, from whom some property in the Armenian Quarter outside the Convent had been purchased, were also outraged at the "false" accusations against Armenians. To prevent any clashes, Abdallah Al Tal positioned Arab Legion guards at the Convent gate.[169]

Hintlian stated that Armenians did not fire a single indiscriminate bullet in 1948 despite being armed for self-defense and ready to defend the community without siding with any of the warring parties.

They had always maintained good neighborly relations with both Arabs and Jews during decades of coexistence. Even at times of intense fighting, this neutrality was manifested in care for human life no matter whether Armenian, Arab or Jew. The main goal in 1948 was to defend their Quarter and reduce human suffering. However, the *Nakba* events and catastrophe that befell Palestinians tilted solidarity towards the plight of Palestinians.

> *"There were ceasefires during the fighting in 1948 and people went out to shop or visit relatives and friends. During one of these lulls, two Jewish men knocked on our door. They were hawkers who went door to door and sold buttons, thread, scissors, and other light goods which they carried in a wooden box. When my mother opened the door, they told her that they were being chased by Arabs and asked to hide in our house. My mother let them in and told the two men to run to the gate of the Vank and to safety before the pursuers caught up with them."[170]*

Disruption of Livelihoods

Armenians in the Armenian Quarter, including the Brotherhood and the laity, found themselves in the crossfire in 1948. Under the leadership of Patriarch Israelian, support from key community members, and a sense of solidarity exhibited by all, the monastery of St. James was spared destruction and the Armenian community that had taken refuge there were relatively protected. It was impossible to fully protect and prevent destruction or loss of life. The location of the Armenian Quarter near the Jewish Quarter and Zion Gate where Jewish fighters were positioned, and the monastery's closeness to the Citadel and Jaffa Gate where the Arab legion had its positions, put the monastery in the theater of combat and resulted in considerable human suffering and material destruction. Abdallah El Tal, the Jordanian Commander stated that Armenians saw themselves as Arabs in 1948, "drank from the same cup" as Palestinians, and lost martyrs in Jerusalem and Jaffa.[171]

Hintlian's father, who was responsible for maintenance work in the Armenian Patriarchate of Jerusalem, stated that for decades post-1948, they were repairing structural damage and cracks caused by the shelling in 1948. Michael Genevisian was eight years old in 1948. He lived in a three-room dwelling with his brother and parents in the Armenian Quarter overlooking the garden of Christ Church. He recalled:

> *"The British have for a few months positioned military officers in the Nammari building 50 meters from our house, using that location as a buffer zone. They were to leave the country on May 15, 1948, but they left two days earlier and the security situation deteriorated by the hour. My father noticed the gathering of men from the Haganah in the building and over the roof top close by the Hovsepian house across from ours. My father and the neighbors were fearful. The whole Armenian Quarter had made it clear that we were Chezok (neutral) with no intention of getting involved in the fighting, yet we were in the middle of the fighting: the battle was in the Armenian Quarter.*

> *"All the Armenian Quarter residents decided to seek shelter in the Armenian Convent. On the night of May 13, my father sneaked into the Christ Church through a gate from our building and approached Reverend Jones, the head of Christ Church, to ask*

if our family could be placed there. Reverend Jones apologized as the place was overcrowded with families from West Jerusalem but offered for us to stay the night and seek elsewhere the next day. We took our mattresses and blankets, and my mother took her jewelry, and we slept in the kitchen at Christ Church.

"The Convent was full so we went to a relative who lived in the Christian Quarter in Haret al Nasara and who had decided to take his family to Zarka[172] in Transjordan after a few days. We ended up having the dwelling for ourselves. When the Jewish Quarter surrendered and the Arab Legion took control on May 28, my father went to check on our house and was shocked by the destruction and rubble everywhere. Only one closet had been spared with its mirror broken. It is possible that other pieces of furniture had been spared but were looted. Vahan Baghsarian told my father that he saw someone carrying our side table and managed to salvage it. My father moved the closet to my uncle Ohannes Genevisian's house.

"With fighting intensifying, mortars falling and ongoing indiscriminate shelling, my parents decided to go to Al Salt like other families who fled to Transjordan. The Razook family was already there, and we were transported by Samuel Chillingirian from Jaffa, who was married to my cousin and had a car which he used to transport people to Jordan and Damascus. The road to Amman was poor; we left via Wadi Shuaib to Al Salt and Sweleh.[173] Living conditions

in Al Salt were quite difficult to say the least and we rented a room from the Qaqeesh family. We ended up with 28 people in the Qaqeesh dwelling, with terrible living conditions, and paying seven dinars per month for a room without a kitchen or bathroom. Imagine 28 people in line to use one bathroom and no running water. A woman used to come every morning with a tin container full of water carried on top of her head and sell it to us for 1.5 piasters. We had no income and none of us were working.

"We lived off the compensation my father had received from the Mandate government as he had been employed at the health department dealing with malaria. We returned to Jerusalem in early January 1949, before the Razook family, to stay in our relatives' house in the Christian Quarter. In February 1949, our relatives returned from Zarqa, and we again had to look for a place to stay. The Armenian Convent was full and we asked the Latin Patriarchate, but priority was for Latins /Catholics. We were given the option to convert to Catholicism but decided not to, although several families did. We went back to the priest at the Armenian Convent, Haigasoon Aprahamian, who asked my father to find an empty room in the Armenian Quarter.

"My father found an empty room across from our previous dwelling. It had cracks in the walls and broken windows, and was not suitable to live in but my father decided that it was much safer than being on the street. We rehabilitated the room and added a kitchen and a restroom in which the four of us lived, *and in which I still live today. One room for four of us for so many years!! The room was very damp and our living conditions were terrible. I became sick with rheumatic fever at a very early age. This affected my schooling at the Armenian school in the Convent. Other larger families also ended up in one room. My cousins, the Terzibashians, a wealthy family of ten, lost four properties in West Jerusalem: two houses near the railway station in lower Baqa'a, one of which still exists although the other was replaced by a three-story building, a third house that still exists in upper Baqa'a with an additional floor added to it, and a fourth property currently housing a yeshiva (Jewish religious school) by Prophets Street in West Jerusalem next to the Ethiopian Church. The whole family ended up in one room in the Convent with almost nothing. For months, my aunt Satenig slept on a chair.*

"My father started looking for a job. We received rations from UNRWA and two meals from the Armenian Convent (lunch and dinner) for some time until meals became available to children only. My father started work as a daily paid employee with the health department (Jordanian government) until he retired in 1962.[174] Our life was never the same again. It was shattered."

There is no estimate of the monetary losses of Palestinian Armenians in property and material losses. Armenians lost over 100 shops and businesses in West Jerusalem due to the division of the city. In the 1930s and early 1940s, Armenian businesses and shops had spread in the Armenian Quarter, the Christian Quarter of the Old City of

Jerusalem, and outside Jaffa Gate in the Princess Mary and Mamilla area. There were some 400 shops in that area, of which about a quarter were run by Armenians and included tailors, grocers, shoe stores, and photographic studios.[175]

Several mechanics and garages

> *"Just outside Jaffa Gate, some 15 shoe polishers and umbrella repairers were lined up opposite Hovannes Berberian's carpet repair shop and the Tossunian fabric store. On the right side of Jaffa Road was Dickranagerdse Bedross, the watch repairer; Krikorian photography (Venus); and Jack Solomon (Studio Paramount). Closer to the Fast Hotel were the Akaian tailors; Vreij Berberian the tailor; Berkho (Hovsepian) vegetable and grocery store; Elia photo studio; and Inglizian and Aprahamian studios. Opposite Barclays Bank was the Tombolakian shoe store with a sign that it would be opening soon in 1948, but it never did. At Princess Mary on the right, there was the shirtmaker Karekin Chekmeyan and Cholackian's Studio Diana. On the left was Zarmar Yerelzian's cigarette store and Ashikian's shoe store (a partner with a Palestinian Arab). A bit farther along was the Mandossian's British Restaurant. In Mamilla, there was Abu Zadig the barber; Arsenian's Grand Pharmacy; Unjian's shoe store; Neshan the cobbler; Aghazarian's Cafe Picadilly; and the Homenetmen Club. There were also several mechanics and garages, including Kehyeyan, Levon Keshishian (Garage Champion), Stamboultsi Aram's garage, Garo's Auto Parts, Unjian's shoe workshop, and Chakmadjian's tile store. Close to the YMCA, was the Sarkissian musical instruments store and Hovsep Mazloom's store."[176]*

Harout Kahvedjian[177] stated: "My father had three stores in 1948 located in the Fast Hotel building, which belonged to the Armenian Patriarchate. The first store was for customer service, on the east side of the building on Jaffa Road, and the other two on the west side on Storrs Avenue were workshops or "dark room" labs for developing, printing, enlarging, and special photo finishing. We lost a house plus three apartments that were rented out. When we sought shelter in the Convent, Dad hired two porters: one carried two mattresses and some comforters, the other carried a small table and four chairs. We left our house with whatever dad and mom could carry in two suitcases; plus the clothes we were wearing. . Dad was able to revive his business in less than two years. He lost the stores in April 1948. In the summer of 1949, he opened a new store in the Christian Quarter where it still stands today."

Maurice Bannayan stated: "My father lost his blacksmith workshop and my uncle Khacho lost his carpentry workshop with all the machinery inside. The same applied to all other Arab and Armenian businesses. Lifelong work was lost overnight. We could not salvage anything. Our parents had to start from scratch and we experienced living conditions we certainly were not used to."[178]

Abcar Zakarian, 98 years of age in 2022 and the oldest living Armenian in the Holy Land, recalls that before 1948 a relatively large Armenian community lived in both Jaffa and Haifa. These families were closely connected with families in Jerusalem and

[handwritten margin note: A relatively large Armenian community lived in both Jaffa and Haifa.]

other Palestinian cities through family ties or friendships. A large percentage of these families fled in 1948 thinking they would soon return after violence subsided. Like Palestinian refugees, they locked their homes and put their house keys in their pocket. The majority fled to Lebanon and could never return, while some went to Jerusalem, Ramallah and Bethlehem. Many moved from Lebanon to Europe, the United States or elsewhere.

> *"I was 25 years old working for Shell in 1948. I was living in the German colony in Haifa with my mother and siblings in a rented apartment in a three-floor building owned by a Christian Arab family. As violence intensified in mid-1948, several Arab and Armenian families were forced to leave, thinking that it would be for a couple of weeks after which they would return to their homes. My mother was adamant that we should not leave. She kept arguing that it might be easy to get to Beirut from Haifa, but we knew no one there, had nowhere to stay, and could end up on the streets after so many people had gone that direction. Most of the residents in my neighborhood left.*

> *"The city was coming fully under Israeli-Jewish control; military personnel were moving from house to house and checking on the residents, obviously looking for those who stayed and those who had left. When they reached our building, they banged on the door. My mother opened the door, they checked our papers, and left to go upstairs. My brother's British passport may have helped. The owner of the building, with a family of 10, told them he was here to stay and would not leave under any circumstances, even if*

Arab Christian family

the whole family were shot. We were relieved as the military personnel left the building and we ended up being two families who stayed in Haifa out of over 20 families in the neighborhood who left. I was relieved as I did not wish to resign from Shell and leave. There were a couple of days when I missed work in May 1948.

"When the war subsided, the structure of employees at work was altered greatly. Before 1948, there were relatively equal numbers of Jews and Arabs (including Armenians) working for the company. When I returned to work, there was only one other Christian Arab and myself in the building with all the Jewish employees." [179]

Others who lost their businesses included Arshag and Khatchig Sarkissian who lost their shoe factory and two retail outlets in Jaffa with over 50 employees. They left everything in 1948, moved to Amman, and never returned. Hovsep Garabedian was a well-known shoemaker in West Jerusalem frequented by clients from neighboring countries. Other prominent craftsmen of the Mandate period who lost their businesses included Boghos Kaplanian, Hagop Krikorian, Tateos Tateossian, Krikor Mnatzaganian, and Kevork Kaplanian.

The family of the master Armenian ceramist Tavit Ohannessian found themselves inside Israel in 1948, while their ceramics workshop was located in the Old City of Jerusalem under Jordanian jurisdiction. Tavit left Palestine with his family exactly thirty years after his arrival in Palestine from Anatolia in 1918. The family was dispersed in Damascus, Cairo and Beirut. Tavit died in Beirut in 1953 and none of his relatives remaining in Israel continued working with ceramics. [180]

Armenian houses in the Armenian Quarter that were shelled in 1948 included: [181]

- The Toumayan house in a residential section.

- The Hovsepian residence opposite the Toumayan house and occupied by Vahan Hovsepian, his wife Sirpoug, and his children Anna and Hovsep.

- The Krakirian house founded on family property in the Christ Church area of Jaffa Gate and close to the Armenian Convent. It was the first house that was blown up and destroyed in the 1948 War.[182]

- The Khatchadourian house.

- The Bedevian house where Anna Bedevian was killed by a sniper bullet from the Dormition Abbey area and where a bomb destroyed the dome of the main room.

- The Genevesian house, next to the Toumayans and close to the shelled house of the Krakirians.

The bombed Krakirian house in 1948. Photo from Antranig Bakerjian's collection.

A bombed Armenian house. Photo from Antranig Bakerjian's collection.

Luckily, most of the residents of these homes had already sought shelter in Christ Church or the Armenian Convent. These houses were not rehabilitated after 1948, mainly due to the losses incurred, lack of money or emigration of residents, and an absence of finance for renovation by the Armenian Convent or the Jordanian government. Scarcity of housing has been a key factor pushing Armenians to emigrate and the Armenian Patriarchs in the 20th century failed to tackle the housing crisis in the Armenian community.[183]

Taking Refuge Elsewhere

Armenians liked the British Mandate period

Genocide survivors who arrived in the Holy Land and many *Kaghakatsi* Armenians witnessed improvements in their lives during the years of the British Mandate prior to the turbulence of 1947-1948. As economic conditions improved, several families followed the trend among Christians and Muslims in the 1930s and 1940s of building or renting homes in the New City area of Jerusalem. In 1905 there were 485 Christian families living in the New City. It is estimated that

2,000 Christians resided outside the city walls in 1914. The movement of families outside the Old City continued into the 1920s and 1930s, including into the Katamon[184] area, and represented social mobility away from shared spaces and extended family dwellings to more modern homes. Christian homes were primarily located near Jaffa Gate, in Baqa'a[185] or Talbiyyeh,[186] Mamilla, Jaffa Road (Manshiyaa), the Musrara area and near Damascus Gate (Mas'udiyya). The less advantaged stayed in the Old City dwellings which lacked the modern amenities of that time.[187]

The new Christian communities outside the Old City constituted a "Christian bloc" along denominational lines with Greeks in one area and Armenians in another, in contrast to Muslims who were divided along clan lines.[188] Several wealthy Armenian families also built villas in Jaffa where Christians were engaged in commerce, especially as the city was located on the coast. They also were involved in construction and the Greek Orthodox Church and Armenians invested heavily in purchasing shops and property. Christians also branched out into agriculture and the purchase of orange groves.[189]

orange groves

Hagop Ramian was a master mason who worked on several buildings in the expanding West Jerusalem, including the lavish villa of Matossian. Hagop lived with his wife and children in a three-story building owned by his wife's uncle, Samuel Shamsi, in Talbiyyeh. His son John Ramian was six years old in 1948 when the family left for Al Salt in Transjordan. The whole family was accommodated in a room rented from Abu Hanna Qaqeesh with a shared kitchen and bathroom with other families. They stayed in Al Salt for six months before returning to a room in the Armenian Quarter given to them by Digin Mariam Dickranagerdsi. They emigrated to the US and Australia in the 1970s. John stated:

> *"A month after June 1967, our Jewish neighbor*
> *from Talbiyyeh came to the Armenian Quarter*

Several wealthy Armenian families also built villas in Jaffa where Christians engaged in commerce.

looking for my parents. Several others came to look for their previous neighbors who lived in the area.... He was greeted by my older brother Artin who was a young man in 1948 and who recognized him. We had a few other visits afterwards until our family emigrated abroad.

"In 1998, I visited our house in Talbiyyeh[190] with my older siblings: George and Mary. George was a graduate of Schneller in 1948. Our walk from the Armenian Quarter to Talbiyyeh was full of emotion and memories, especially for George who could remember some streets and buildings. We passed the YMCA, reached the building, and knocked at a door. A woman, Naomi, opened the door and immediately recognized George after 50 years. 'You are George," she said. 'You used to play the accordion when you were young, and I used to bother you.' It took George some time to remember but Naomi's memory was sharper. We looked around and left with bitterness; we never had the chance to revisit. In some encounters with Samuel Shamsi, my father used to say 'Kasartilli Dahri lama Tli3na min Altalbiyyeh' (You broke my back when we left Talbiyyeh (in Arabic)). Obviously, it was a hard ride for my father afterwards." [191]

John worked in Libya in 1964, emigrated to the US in 1969, and lived there until 2015 when he returned to Amman.

In 1948 several families abandoned and lost their homes (owned or rented) to the advancing Jewish militias, becoming refugees, some for the second time since the Armenian Genocide. The Patriarchate was again deluged with Armenians who required shelter and assistance because they had lost everything.[192] Overnight in 1948, Armenian communities of 10,000 in Haifa and Jaffa shrank to just 1,000, with many taking refuge in Beirut and Amman. Several of the most affluent Armenians lost their houses in 1948.

Some of the abandoned homes were mansions by today's standards and were built as monuments to be preserved. Several still stand proudly today, occupied by others, while the owners are denied entry. These mansions are testament to a history that cannot be wiped. The mansion of Paul Lazaros in the German Colony in West Jerusalem was turned into a nature museum. Lazaros was one of the richest and most prominent merchants and art collectors of the early 1900s in Palestine. One of the stones of his building still has a carving in Armenian.

The Lazaros house in the German Colony in West Jerusalem.
Photo by the author.

Khatchadour Tateosian lost his large house on the main highway to Jaffa, as did Frederick Murad (Muradian). These houses attest to the size and beautiful architecture of the construction at that time.[193]

Ohannes Krikorian was from a well-to-do family of merchants and agricultural landowners in Jaffa. He took refuge in Ramallah, leaving everything behind, and lived in Ramallah until he passed away.

Armenian writing on the entrance of the Lazaros house. Photo by the author

Aram Krikorian, a civil engineer and licensed surveyor with the British government, and his wife Nevart Kalaydjian left their house which had been built in 1880 by Aram's grandfather Hagop and his brother Soghmon on two plots of land. Vahan Krikorian who lived on the second floor of the house also left. Aram went to Amman and Beirut.[194]

Dr. Krikorian, Aram Krikorians cousin, also lived with his extended family, including aunts and uncles, in Baqa'a. Krikor Krikorian was a medical officer in the Turkish Army in 1914 and Deputy Chief Medical Officer in the Palestine Government of the British Mandate years. On June 16, 1948, Jewish forces took complete control of Baqa'a; nearly every house was empty. Krikor and the rest of the family first moved to the Armenian Convent, then to Beirut where Krikor became head of laboratories at the American University of Beirut hospital for the rest of his working years.

Matossian was an orphan raised in Schneller[195] and became one of the richest Armenians in Jerusalem. The family lost their villa in Talbiyyeh.

*The Matossian house
in Talbiyyeh, West
Jerusalem.
Photo by the author.*

*A stone of the Matossian
house in Hebrew language.
The inscription states that
the Matossian house was
built in 1927.
Photo by the author.*

The Gulvanessians used to live in the German Colony and settled in Nicosia in 1948, moving from there to the United Kingdom in the 1960s.

The Markarians lived on Princess Mary Avenue close to the Jewish neighborhood of Nachlat Shiva. The area was becoming increasingly dangerous with ongoing clashes between Jews and Arabs, so the Markarians moved to the Katamon area in 1947. They were soon forced to leave without enjoying their new residence and abandoned all their belongings following the bombing of the Semiramis Hotel in January 1948.[196]

The Karakashian family had purchased a house in Katamon in 1947 but lost the house even before moving into it. They spent two months in the Armenian Convent during the 1948 War and then moved to Amman. They returned to live behind their shop on Nablus Road in 1950 and then moved into a building in Shu'fat in 1954. [197]

In his memoir, John Rose refers to the day after the bombing of the Semiramis Hotel: "*Looking across the open fields towards the main Katamon Road, I saw crowds of civilians weighed down with belongings, hurrying in a state of disarray and panic to escape to the relative safety of the Old City -- a mass exodus of civilians fleeing the ravages of war. It was not only Arab residents who were on the move but Armenians, Greeks and others.*"

Apraham Hagopian, whose family lived in Talbiyyeh, took refuge in a crammed room in the Armenian Quarter.

The Toumayan family left their house in Katamon for the Armenian Convent and then went to Amman for three years. The father returned to Jerusalem to see how he could bring the family back but became ill and died. This prompted the whole family of eight (a pregnant mother, three daughters and four sons) to come to live in one room in the Armenian Quarter.[198]

Der Bedrossian took refuge in East Jerusalem, later moved to Ramallah, and then emigrated abroad. Maurice, Abcar Bannayan's son, was 11 years old in 1948. Maurice stated:

"My father, mother and my three siblings lived in Katamon. My father Abcar Bannayan was a master blacksmith. We had other Armenian neighbours: a Voskeritchian, Joseph Sahagian, and my maternal grandparents the Sultanians, as well as our cousins the Manougians. Our Arab neighbors living on the second floor were the family of judge Khoury. Next door were also the family of Dr. Freij, Damiani and Kassissieh.

"With the intensifying clashes and after the bombing of the Semiramis hotel on January 5, 1948, which was close to our house, my father decided we should move to a house we had in the Armenian Quarter where one of my uncles was living. My paternal grandparents and my aunt living with them also left at the same time, and so did my aunt's family who was married into the Mustaklem family. My parents went back a couple of times to get some stuff from the house but it was unsafe. From a luxury home with several bedrooms, we moved to one bedroom where we stayed for a couple of months. My family then moved to Damascus for a few months to seek work but soon returned to Amman where we settled until we emigrated abroad.

"My father went back to visit our house through the Mandelbaum Gate in 1949. His previous Jewish business friends, the Zilbersteins, accompanied him. He reached the house to find it was occupied by more than one family. He pleaded to go inside but his friend told him it was pointless because all the valuable things would be gone. He was keen to see the piano he

had bought for his daughter which to him had a very sentimental value. It was impossible to check.

"My two aunts from my father's side (Naze married to Aghabekian and Martha married to Manoogian) and their families also left their houses in Baqa'a, as did one of my mother's brothers Garabed and my father's brother Khacho Bannayan. They all left everything and fled to the Armenian Quarter. A journey from wealth to nothing."

Photo provided by Maurice Bannayan in the mid-1940s. In the center is Maurice's grandfather, Kevork Bannayan, with his grandmother from the Mazloom family sitting next to Maurice. Nectar Bannayan, Maurice's cousin, is seated to the right of Maurice and her grandfather.

George /Kevork Aghabekian and his wife Nazouhi and children had to leave their spacious home and move into a barely ventilated room in the Armenian Quarter; they lost everything and were impoverished. They were accommodated in one of the dwellings around the *Hakourah* (garden) and in which other displaced families from West Jerusalem had taken refuge. The *Hakourah* was an area for recreation in which they could breathe and escape from the ancient, crammed dwellings in which they were forced to live.

Dr. Vahan Kalbian was a renowned Armenian doctor in Jerusalem from the mid-1910s and a graduate from AUB. He worked in the Negev and served as a medical officer in the Russian Compound in Jerusalem (the *Moscobiyyeh* in Arabic). He became the private doctor of the High Commissioner and his official guests. Vahan lived with his wife and four children in Talbiyyeh. He lost their house and a personal library with a vast collection of medical and other books. He never saw the library collection again.[199]

In 1948 Hagop Melikian and his family fled from their home and left behind his private library with dozens of books, including a complete German-translated set of Shakespeare plays and a 19th-century German encyclopedia.[200]

The well-to-do Merguerian family sought shelter in the Convent in 1948 after leaving their house in West Jerusalem. They were offered a room and their son went to their house in West Jerusalem to collect some items, but found himself unable to return. He appealed to the Israeli authorities and eventually managed to bring his parents back from the Convent to their house in West Jerusalem through the Mandelbaum passage. The family was reunited and ultimately stayed in West Jerusalem.[201]

Hagop Terzibashian (initially Manougian) was a very wealthy and well-established tailor who was one of the first residents to move out of the Armenian Quarter. He built and owned four houses in the new suburbs of Jerusalem and lived in the affluent neighborhood of Katamon with other Armenian and Arab families. Michael Genevisian stated he remembers the days when he used to visit his maternal cousins, the Terzibashians, in West Jerusalem.

> *"One of the Terzibashian properties still stands today and is located close to the old railway station in lower Baqa'a. After 1967, my cousins (the owners) and I went to check the area. The house had, of course, been taken by its new tenants. We remembered how the house was divided, the details of the dwelling, and where my aunts used to sleep. The eucalyptus tree was also there. We could not enter the house but peeked in from outside. It was difficult and unexplainable."*[202]

Others who lost homes included Mukhtarian, Sarkis Boyadjian, the brothers Azad and Garbis, Taniel Markarian, Yeghsapet and Michael Elian, and the Dikranians. A dozen Armenian families who lived in Joret Al Ennab[203] just outside Jaffa Gate and several families living in Abu Tor [204] also fled their homes.[205]

As a young adolescent myself after 1967, I vividly remember when my father took me and my younger brother to walk around Talbiyyeh and see the mansions owned by Palestinian Arabs and Armenians. We were fascinated by the structures but were too young to relate to what my father mumbled as we moved from one street to the other. We took that walk a couple of times. As the years passed, I could relate more and more to the pain and self-pity expressed by my father while staring at those houses and the wounded memories he carried as we walked back along Jaffa Road towards Jaffa Gate. These words were also echoed in a discussion with Garo Gosdigian who remembered the same walks he took as a child with his father and his brother, where his father pointed to them were several Armenian families lived before 1948.[206]

Armenians who lost property in what became the State of Israel and who were displaced did not experience being refugees like the Armenians survivors of the Genocide, nor did they end up in refugee camps like the Palestinian refugees, although they shared experiences of poverty, anxiety, and helplessness. Most ended up internally displaced in the Armenian Convent or the Armenian Quarter, or in Lebanon and Amman supported by the Armenian communities there. They were not orphaned as many of the Genocide survivors had been but were intact families of refugees. For some, their abandoned houses in the fashionable suburbs of Katamon, Baqa'a, and the German and Greek Colonies were soon listed under an absentee property law[207]and transferred to Jews. One can only imagine the experience of losing your residence and possessions overnight, and knowing that they were given to a stranger while you are stripped of your dignity and way of life. Those who had the chance to visit their homes after 1967 have generally spoken of feeling oppression, cruelty, pain, bitterness and helplessness. Some regretted making the visit.[208]

Alice Zakarian was a young adolescent in 1948 and recalled the difficult times in an interview:

> *"We were living in a rented home in Ramleh in 1948 owned by an Arab family. The head of the family worked with my father in the railway station. We used to hear that fighting between Arab and Jewish fighters was more intense in Ramleh than in other cities such as Haifa. One day we were all asked to leave our homes open and gather in an open garage space. We did and were left with no food or drinks for many hours. When we returned home, everything was upside down; they had obviously been looking for weapons.*
>
> *"Most Armenian families in Ramleh at the time left in fear of their lives like the Arab families. My family*

*and probably a couple of other Armenian families
remained out of over 20 families. The majority
went to Jerusalem to stay in the Armenian
Convent. I remember Dr. Bodossian drove his car
to Jerusalem. On the way near Latrun, Bodossian's
car was stopped and taken away from him, and
he made his way to Jerusalem on foot. A nurse,
Vehanoush Aivazian, also went to Jerusalem.*

*"After the fall of Ramleh, my 16-year-old brother was
detained for nine months. We knew nothing about
him. When he was released, we hardly recognized
him. Despite everything, I have great memories
of Ramleh. There were neighborhoods of different
religions: Christians, Muslim clans like the Fanous
or Sakakini, Armenians and others...this was all
devastated."*[209]

Around three to four thousand people from all over Palestine were
accommodated by the Armenian Patriarchate of Jerusalem in the
Convent. Some stayed with families outside the Convent or were
accommodated elsewhere in convents, schools and hospitals with
support from non-governmental organisations and international
agencies. For example, the Poshoghlians from Katamon, Bahjians
from Jaffa Road, Nazar Karijian and Hossep Keshishian from
Musrara, and Demirgian and Manuel Chomikian stayed at the Casa
Nova in Jerusalem where the accommodation was not free of charge.
A monthly sum was paid for each room by the occupant.[210]

For many refugees, their lives were shattered in 1948 with the loss
of property and possessions. Thanks to support from the Armenian
Patriarchate of Jerusalem and extended families in the Old City or
elsewhere such as Amman and Beirut, and combined with a sense

of industriousness and drive to start again from scratch, many rose to prominence and made major contributions to their host countries.

CHAPTER FIVE

LOSS OF PROPERTY, DISPLACEMENT AND THE SAGA OF A SECOND REFUGE TO MANY ARMENIANS

After WWII, there were four major waves of Armenian emigration from Palestine.[211]

- The first was *Nerkaght* (emigration in Armenian). Between 1946 and 1949, a mass post-war immigration drive sought to repatriate Armenians to Soviet Armenia. Around 90,000 took up the offer. These were families expelled and displaced from their homes in the former Ottoman Empire during the Armenian Genocide. Those from the Middle East boarded ships in Beirut looking for the Armenian homeland, even if it was not independent then. This historical event was known as the *Nergakht*.

- The second was due to the 1948 War.

- The third wave took place in 1955 when George Mardigian of the Armenian National Committee for Homeless Armenians (ANCHA) visited Jerusalem. He was keen to encourage Armenians from various countries to emigrate to the United States and start a new life in a place with greater opportunities. He facilitated the acquisition of US visas through his contacts. George focused on *Homenetmen* club members and within a couple of years, many of the club leaders and regular members had left Jerusalem. As a result, the club declined and lost some of its clout.

- The fourth wave took place following the 1967 War.

- Emigration was always ongoing, but these four waves had the most destructive impact on the community.

Refuge, Displacement and Shattered Memories

Thousands of Palestinian refugees, including Armenian Palestinians, became stateless after 1948.[212] Nearly 7000 Armenians took refuge in nearby Arab countries while around 3000 others resorted to the Convent. Armenians experienced being refugees on two occasions: the Armenian Genocide and in 1948. Although they did not establish refugee camps, they became refugees in church-related institutions and fully experienced loss, devastation, poverty, and unemployment like refugees elsewhere.

Several factors prompted people to emigrate and leave years of family history behind. Some left for study abroad or were offered an employment opportunity and opted not to return. Others seeking better opportunities were encouraged by family members or acquaintances who had already emigrated. Others left because of financial difficulties, the political environment, and the lack of a stable horizon. Some opted to stay even as internally displaced people.

The Terzibashian family fled in 1948 from Katamon to the Armenian Convent, then from Jerusalem to Amman, then back to the Armenian Convent and ultimately migration abroad. This could be the story of several other families who moved from abundance to poverty, with loss of life due to the stress of the challenges they faced.

David Terzibashian eloquently summed up the difficulties and suffering undergone by many Armenians after 1948 due to displacement:

> *"I became a refugee while in my mother's womb in 1948. My grandfather, aunts, parents, and siblings*

took refuge in the Armenian Convent, leaving our properties behind in West Jerusalem with barely anything with us. After a short time at the Convent, my grandfather took the family to Jordan looking for a better life. It was so difficult to shoulder responsibility for a large refugee family after living in abundance.

"*He had a massive heart attack on the day he rented a new residence for his family after formerly being a property owner. He passed away in Amman and the family had to transport him at vast cost to be buried in Jerusalem as he wished. My father Hagop honored his father's wishes and with his cousin Mgerdich (Meger) Bedevian and Asadour Antreassian's help, they took the body to Jerusalem at enormous risk and cost.*

"*Once the body arrived in Jerusalem, it was not possible to bury him at the Armenian St. Saviour Cemetery on Mount Zion as it was already under Jewish control and inaccessible to Armenians. He was buried at the Keeraj Khana in the Armenian Convent with other victims of war at the time. My grandfather's death prompted the family to return from Jordan to the same single room at the Armenian Convent. This return took place soon after I was born. In 1956 the family was offered an additional room as some rooms became vacant when Armenian families left for the US. We stayed there until most of us emigrated abroad over the next three decades. "I had five aunts, three of whom were single. One of my aunts, Mariam, was 40 years old in 1948.*

She was not married as my father had believed that those courting my aunts were interested in the family wealth. Like the rest of the family, Mariam had lived a comfortable life prior to 1948 in a spacious house. Once the family was forced to take refuge in the Armenian Convent, she was living in one room accommodating over 10 family members with zero privacy and dreadful living conditions. The situation was so challenging that she eventually lost her mind. One day, she tried to run through a fence near Zion Gate to go back home. Her clothes caught on the barbed wire and she was rescued and returned to the Armenian Convent."[213]

Yeghia Missislian lived in a Patriarchate property in the Armenian Quarter. Yeghia had held a senior position at the post office during the British Mandate; he was highly educated and was fluent in several languages. He could also play the violin. According to a relative, he lived like a king but became unemployed in 1948. He soon became an alcoholic and committed suicide in the mid-1950s at his residence in the Armenian Quarter where he lived with his mother.[214] There are a couple of other Armenians who committed suicide after their losses in 1948.

It is believed that two-thirds of Armenians in the Holy Land were forced to flee in 1948. Several families initially left for Jordan, Syria or Lebanon, but often moved on elsewhere. Cyprus was one of the destinations where several Armenian families from Jerusalem, Jaffa and Haifa settled.

Garabed and Araxy Mihranian moved from Jerusalem to Cyprus in 1948, the first people to leave. They were followed by the Gulvanessians who settled in Nicosia in 1948, moving from there to the United Kingdom in the 1960s. Haygaz Azadian from Jerusalem also settled in Cyprus.

Boghous and Yevkine Aintablian and their children, plus Armen Aintablian and his wife Haigouhi Yenovkian left for Cyprus in 1950. In 1948, Pauline, Yevkine (with husband Boghos) and their children (Vazken, Varoujan and Suzie) left for Jordan, then to Lebanon and Cyprus. They lost everything in Cyprus and were forced to leave in 1974 with the Turkish invasion of Nicosia. They moved to Beirut but left to the US following the outbreak of civil war in Lebanon. In half a century, the two sisters had experienced deportation, loss of family, and multiple migrations and dispossession.

The 1948 period was a turning point. Despite economic deterioration, there was building and expansion by Armenians. Some participated in defending their Quarter but were not engaged in politics like other Christians or affiliated with any specific party.[215] The Armenian community remained mostly neutral throughout the time of the Mandate. Although it was a dramatic period, it brought unity to the Armenian community of Palestine at large and a sense of duty towards the larger Palestinian community.

The Armenian Quarter found itself in the crossfire in 1948 because of its location between the Jewish and the Arab Legion positions. Patriarch Israelian took the lead and the Patriarchate provided shelter, food, and clothing for all who had left their towns due to the bombardment of their homes. He succeeded in salvaging the Monastery of St. James from destruction by leaving it out of the theater of combat. However, the Armenian Quarter suffered considerable human and material losses. The Patriarchate coordinated with laity within and outside the Convent to pull things together and defend the population and the Old City (Jaffa Gate area in particular). My father Ohannes recalled these times:

"The immediate aftermath of 1948 was hard on the Armenian community and the larger Palestinian community in general. Armenians were grappling with the death of loved ones, rehabilitation of injuries, reconstruction and rehabilitation of destroyed physical structures, and attending to the needs of internally displaced Armenian refugees from what became Israel. Additionally, there was a family and brain drain by people leaving Palestine seeking better opportunities elsewhere. The Jewish Quarter residences next to our homes were hard hit and the Jerusalem population in general was drained after months of fighting. Although it was hard to see some of our wealthy relatives lose everything and grapple to make ends meet, despite all the challenges we were determined to pull the community together, accept our pain, and move on. It is very hard to explain the feeling. I always wonder how things would have been now if the tragic events of 1948 had not taken place."[216]

From Dikran Bakerjian's collection. The Kaghakatsi band in around 1950, including Antranig Bakerjian, Murad Muradian, and Hagop Zakarian, with community members gathering around the bombed house where Anna Bedevian was killed by a sniper bullet.

For some Armenians, there was an inevitable identity crisis. Those who stayed in what became Israel lost their Palestinian citizenship and became 'Israeli Armenians" in a new situation and in a newly created country. For most of them it was a second experience of being a refugee and they lost many of their community members and severed family ties. Sarkis Keroghlanian, for example, an Armenian chef of the French Consul General, stayed in West Jerusalem while his wife and children stayed in the Convent in East Jerusalem. If it were not for the Mandelbaum Gate[217] and the short yearly visit he was permitted to East Jerusalem, Sarkis would not have been able to physically be with his family for the following 19 years. He would have had to resort to waving at his family from the rooftop of the French Hospital opposite New Gate with his family on the top of the Freres Boys School inside New Gate. Other families such as the Krikorians became Israelis because they stayed in Jaffa, Haifa and Ramleh rather than seeking refuge in the areas under Jordanian rule.

The *Nakba* marked the uprooting of many Armenians from their properties and businesses, particularly in West Jerusalem, and the coastal towns and cities of what had been mandatory Palestine. After the 1948 War, Palestinians who fled or were forcefully expelled from their ancestral homeland found shelter in ill-prepared refugee camps in surrounding Arab countries. Alongside them were Armenians who sought refuge in Lebanon, Syria or Jordan. Armenians from all over Palestine came to the Armenian Quarter of Jerusalem's Old City for safety and shelter. The *Nakba* was an economic and physical catastrophe for Armenians in Palestine. Their Armenian Quarter suffered the most damage compared to the other three quarters of the Old City and the maintenance department of the Armenian Patriarchate had to deal with structural cracks for many years. The issue of Palestinian refugees due to the partition of Palestine in 1947, and the ensuing battles on the ground with the Jewish fighters who took over Palestinian villages, is one of the most important, complex and unresolved in modern history.

The Disconnect of Armenian Families and Communities After the Palestinian *Nakba*

The 1948 Arab-Israeli War severed ties and disconnected Armenian communities in Palestine. The Armenians of Jaffa, Lydda, Ramleh, Nazareth and Haifa were reduced to a small fraction as the total Palestinian community lost two-thirds of the population. Some Armenians in Palestine became refugees for the second time. Their properties were confiscated by the Israeli government and were put under the control of the Custodian of Absentee Properties. The Armenian community of over 15,000 in the Holy Land was damaged by the British withdrawal from Palestine and the creation of the State of Israel in 1948.

Nearly all Armenians in the coastal towns (Jaffa and Haifa) and the New City (West Jerusalem) fled to the walled monastery in the Old City or abroad for safety. The Armenian communities of Jaffa and Haifa, which numbered ten thousand, were reduced to a mere 1,000 people. Only one-tenth of the Armenian population in Jaffa, Haifa and West Jerusalem remained in what became Israel, and the number of Armenians in Palestine dropped to 5,000 in 1949 and 3500 prior to 1967.[218] Many activities in the Armenian community ceased, including the work of the HEM Young Ladies Committee which was established in 1942 but stopped work in 1948.[219] The two kindergarten and elementary level Armenian schools, the Gelkhatir School in Jaffa with 330 students and the St Yeghia School in Haifa with 280 students in 1945, both closed down.[220]

In West Jerusalem, several hundred Armenian families lost their homes and businesses as part of the forced exodus of Palestinian refugees. Like the Palestinian Arabs of 1948, many Armenian families lost their homes to the advancing Israeli army in Jerusalem only to find themselves refugees once more. The once-prosperous Armenians found themselves crammed into rooms in the Saint James Convent. Many became stateless in Beirut or moved later to Europe and the States. As the Patriarchate allotted much of its resources to accommodate over 3,000 new refugees in 1948, its financial capacity was drained. At the end of the war, the Armenian Church in Palestine had lost over 50% of its members.

Those who fled to nearby countries were forced to reconstitute their lives in exile. There are no estimates of the value of the properties lost by Armenians or of their non-material losses and sentimental memories, in addition to the trauma carried by dispossessed refugees who lacked capital to rebuild their lives. The emigration of some of the most able and educated constituted a brain drain for both the Armenian and Palestinian communities.[221]

> *"Our life in the years after 1948 was very difficult. After I became sick, I lost many school days and years. The community lost several family members, neighbors and friends who emigrated in the 1950s and 1960s. Our neighbors, the Haig Khachadourian family, left for Beirut in 1948 where Haig became a professor at Haigazian University.*
>
> *"My uncle Ohannes Genevisian moved to Amman. His son Tavit worked for TWA and later held a high position, while his brother Barkev ended up in New Jersey. Dr. Pascal left for Beirut and many others left. Life was not the same and the loss of community members has continued until today with very few left.*

*"I have never given up, I taught myself languages and
became a local guide. That is what kept me going.
Several of my childhood friends who ended up in
Canada, the US and Australia make it a point to
visit often. I most enjoy these visits as it brings back
memories of our childhood. Yes, those were difficult
days but most cherished. I do wonder what life would
have been like had all these people stayed." [222]*

When Palestinian citizenship ceased to exist at the end of the
British Mandate in Palestine and the creation of Israel in 1948,
Armenians who remained in the cities that became Israeli (Ramleh,
Jaffa, Haifa, and Nazareth) obtained Israeli citizenship. Those who
stayed in the West Bank and in East Jerusalem, or who took refuge
there, fell under the administered areas of the Hashemite Kingdom
of Jordan and were given Jordanian passports (travel documents
and not citizenship). Those who stayed in the Gaza Strip fell under
the administered areas of Egypt but were not offered Egyptian
citizenship. Thus, Armenians ended up living under three different
juridical regimes. It became of the utmost importance for the Church
to organize personal status matters and protection of its members.

The village of Atlit had around 20 Armenian families (140 people
descendants of Armenian Genocide survivors from Adana).
Armenians lived in one of three distinct areas of Atlit southeast of
the castle. Atlit was attacked several times in early 1948 and was
occupied on May 15, 1948. Its inhabitants were pressured to evacuate
because of the attacks.[223] Although some Armenian families stayed
in Atlit post-1948, they faced several problems including lack of
connection to the electricity grid, proper sewage and drinking water.
The state continued to deprive the population of these facilities until
the residents were eventually forced to leave. The last Armenian left
Atlit in 1981 and the "only Armenian village in Israel was lost." The

residents were not overtly forced to leave but, as a previous resident stated: "Politically, they made it hard for us so we would be unable to stay there."[224]

In the opening foreword of the Armenian Patriarchate's *Sion* magazine in January 1949, Patriarch Israelian wrote on the division of Palestine, the difficult situation in the city of Jerusalem, and the deteriorating economic and political situation. He referred to 700,000 Palestinians becoming refugees and thanked the Jordanian army and King Abdullah I. He expressed gratitude to the Catholicos of all Armenians who had ordered prelacies worldwide to aid Palestinian Armenians. He also thanked the Catholicos of Cilicia who had raised funds and sent medicine to the Patriarchate. He was grateful to the AGBU and the Gulbenkian Foundation who helped the Palestinian Armenian community to remain steadfast. He stated that the tragedies in 1948 had made many Armenians into refugees but Armenians remained in the Holy Land. He described families who had sold almost everything they had to keep their families alive and who were living in very poor dwellings that were "uninhabitable" with darkness and damp. He called upon the diaspora to continue fundraising and aid to the Patriarchate in Jerusalem and its Armenian community. The *Sion* magazine's editors in that same issue alluded to the tragedy that befell Palestinians, including Armenians, with suffering everywhere and a dark future ahead.

The Patriarchate entered 1949 with grave financial difficulties. The first Christmas in January[225] after the war was painful after a whole year of violence and very poor economic conditions. It is a tradition that on Christmas morning, the Armenian community is served *Khashlamah* at the Nativity Convent. Men gather to eat with the priests and then greet the Patriarch with Christmas wishes. There was no money to buy meat and Mehran Kalaydjian, one of the wealthier Armenian merchants in Jerusalem at the time who ran the cracked wheat business just outside the Armenian Convent, offered the ox used to move the huge wheat cracker stone. Kevork Kukeyan shot the ox and it is said that Armenians who had not had meat for over a year ate meat for two consecutive days.[226]

It is clear that the Armenian Patriarchate of Jerusalem was the address where most Armenians sought a place of refuge. The majority of the around three thousand internally displaced refugees who arrived at St. James Convent and the Armenian Quarter eventually emigrated. Living conditions were very poor as the Convent was overcrowded and large families were accommodated in one room. As children started to grow up, it was impossible for families to live in such a challenging living environment. Eventually, most emigrated to Syria, Lebanon, Armenia or the west through Jordan.[227] Armenian demographic devastation is reflected in the demographic figures before and after 1948.

Regardless of the living conditions at the Convent, David Terzibashian wonders what would have happened to his family had it not been for the shelter they were given there after losing their properties in West Jerusalem and their lives being turned upside down.

> *"The Terzibashians were a very wealthy and well-established family of tailors. They were among the first residents to move out of the Armenian Quarter of the Old City, and they built four houses in the new suburbs of Jerusalem. In 1948 my family was living in the affluent neighborhood of Katamon next to other Armenian and Arab families. The family lived in a beautiful house in which three of my siblings lived with my grandfather and three aunts. It became dangerous to stay in Katamon as the Haganah with Palmach reinforcements were operating in the*

neighborhood. My grandfather Apraham was injured by mortar shrapnel in his leg and needed special medical attention because he was a diabetic. We lost three buildings overnight. The room given to us at the Convent accommodated 10 people, including my pregnant mother, my father, my injured grandfather, my siblings and my three aunts.

"*Despite the poor living conditions at the Convent compared to what the family had owned previously, we were grateful that we were together as a family under one roof. However, the years after 1948 were dreadful for my family. Life was not the same for my parents and aunts. The family soon lost my grandfather, the backbone of the family. We were crammed in a room at the Armenian Convent on top of the church. We were also close to the common toilet area watching people queue throughout the day. The smell was awful. Bed bugs had a feast on us at night.*

"*While living on top of the church, the nights were scary when the bodies of those who died were kept in the church before burial the next day. As children, we were scared knowing that a dead body was lying under us.*[228] *There was no privacy for bathing. We were lucky to be able to go to the hammam to bathe once a week. As the days passed, the space allotted to our family by the Convent was shrinking as we were growing up and our special needs as adolescents were increasing. My brothers and older sister Vartouhi later moved to settle in the US in the late 1960s and early 1970s. My younger sister, Isgouhi, lives in Ramleh, Israel.*"

During 1948, of a total of 10,000 residents left in the Old City, 6,000 were Armenians. While they defended their Quarter, they suffered considerable damage from the *Haganah* shelling of the Old City and forty civilians lost their lives with another 250 wounded.[229]

There were several reasons for the decline in the fortunes of the Armenian Patriarchate of Jerusalem and the community from the events of 1948. Discord within the religious Brotherhood significantly undermined the Patriarchate, especially after the death of Israelian in October 1949. Some of its members defrocked and left the Patriarchate. Conflicts in the Patriarchate regarding the election of Israelian's successor dominated Armenian religious and secular life.

Armenians from Jaffa, Haifa and Nazareth who used to visit relatives or friends in Jerusalem, and Ramallah, Bethlehem, Beit Jala, and Jericho in the winter months, ceased to come. Ironically, some of those who had once been visitors fled from their homes in Jaffa and Haifa to become refugees in Jerusalem and Ramallah, for example the Baghbouderians in Jerusalem, the Minassians (Minas) in Gaza, and the Shanlikians and Kevorkians in Ramallah. A few continued to come to Jerusalem and Bethlehem on brief trips at Christmas through the Mandelbaum Gate.

> *"We used to come to Jerusalem whenever we were granted a permit to cross the Mandelbaum Gate for a 24-hour stay for Christmas. We could not get a permit on a yearly base and we were sometimes denied; I guess they had a quota of a specific number permitted passage. We used to stay with my aunt who was married into the Babigian family. The permitted duration of the stay was so short that we used to pray that Christmas falls on a Friday so that we could get to stay an additional day because of*

> *the Sabbath.* " [230]
> *"One of my brothers passed through the Mandelbaum*
> *Gate and while trying to assist another passenger, he*
> *mixed Armenian with Hebrew. This got him into*
> *trouble on the eastern side and the Armenian*
> *Patriarchate of Jerusalem had to intervene to ensure*
> *his release.* "[231]

Following the partition of Palestine, Patriarch Israelian expressed his concern for the welfare of his people and his concern for the holy sites. In the Seventeenth Meeting of the United Nations Conciliation Commission for Palestine Committee on Jerusalem, held in the Old City in the presence of the Patriarchs of Jerusalem, Israelian[232] opened the conversation with a detailed account of the historical relationship between the Armenians and the people of Palestine. He stated that he was satisfied with the existing situation in Arab-held territory but was anxious to know what had happened to the property of the Armenian Church, including in Jerusalem: the monastery erected on the site of the House of Caiaphas was particularly important to the Armenian Church as it was the only cemetery of all the Armenian Patriarchs and is formally recognized as a holy site; the extensive land behind Barclays Bank on which shops had been erected and rented out to Jews; in Jaffa, the Armenian Church, monastery and school; properties in Haifa; and a monastery in Ramleh.[233] He also expressed his wish to see the fifth century mosaic outside Damascus Gate as it was the property of the Armenian Church. He pointed to the considerable sufferings and losses in Jaffa and Haifa, and asked for people to be allowed to return to Haifa, Jaffa and Ramleh. He pointed out that Armenians had numbered 10,000 at the time of the partition, and that during the hostilities, the Patriarchate had been under fire for several days, but he had advised the 3,000-strong Armenian population of Jerusalem not to evacuate the city.

A summary of the Patriarch's requests included provisions in a future constitution to safeguard the interests of Christians as a whole, and the rights and privileges of the different confessions attained through efforts and sacrifices during many centuries, and respect for the Status Quo. Additionally, Christians should be allowed to return to the holy sites. The Patriarch stressed that his attempts to have Jerusalem declared an open city had failed.

Armenians in Palestine continued to be one of the three major Christian communities (Greek, Latin and Armenian) controlling the main holy and pilgrimage sites in the Holy Land via the Brotherhood of St. James, which was made up of around 50 members. The aftermath of 1948 brought further tensions within the Brotherhood. Tensions have arisen periodically within the Patriarchate/Brotherhood over Patriarchal elections. Tensions cooled with the arrival of Patriarch Torkom Manougian in 1990.[234]

Moving on and Rising Again

Between 1948 and 1967, Armenians were well-positioned among the Arab Palestinian population. Second and third generation Armenian descendants of Genocide survivors were accustomed to living in their second home. Armenians taught in Arab schools, worked as public servants with the Jordanian government or prospered as merchants and shopkeepers throughout the Old City, outside the walls, and in Ramallah and Bethlehem. Despite the detrimental consequences of 1948 on the demography and geography of the country and the direct and indirect forced exodus of people, the breakup of their country, economic depression, political instability, unemployment, lack of local schools of higher learning, and their miniscule numbers, innumerable Armenian Jerusalemites pulled their boots up, and achieved success locally and abroad.

> *"Although in political turmoil and economic depression [high unemployment], the period between 1950 to 1955 marked the cultural glory period of Armenian Jerusalem. Every year, the Hoyetchmen Club organized bazaars, presented plays, had piano concerts, stand-up comedy nights, "teeya seghan" (Tea Evenings), women's cultural evenings (men not allowed), panakhousoutune (lectures). The club -- I think together with the Kaghakatsis -- sponsored a tightrope show and presented an Armenian kamancha player from Lebanon. There were other cultural programs but I cannot remember because I was young then. Our family was Hoyetchmen so I am familiar with the club's activities. I am sure Homenetmen was similarly active. Likewise, Paresirats screened movies because there were no cinemas. Paresisrats also sponsored bazaars and plays ("vartanants") and hosted tarkmanchats graduation ceremonies."[235]*

Maurice Bannayan summarized what his parents went through after becoming refugees:

> *"It was torture to go from abundance to very little and not knowing what the future would bring. It hurt my parents a lot not to be able to meet the family's needs. Thankfully, my father and his brothers worked very hard in Amman. They were skilled carpenters and blacksmiths and were able to recover. We all did very well; the suffering prompted us all to work harder. It was not easy but we made it – all of us."*

Master Armenian ceramists continued to produce quality ceramics using techniques passed down from one generation to another. The beautiful tiles decorating some of the old homes and villas of East and West Jerusalem abandoned by Palestinians in 1948 were the work of Armenian ceramists. Tavit Ohannessian produced most of his beautiful ceramics work in the 30 years after his arrival in Palestine up to 1948 and is considered the father of traditional Armenian hand-painted ceramics in Palestine. The Balians still have their pottery factory known as "Palestinian Pottery" on Nablus Road where four generations of Balian ceramists have created beautiful ceramics that are traded worldwide. Items and murals from the factory have travelled to homes across the world and the work of the Balians has received much press coverage. The Karakashians also retain their workshop in the Old City and continue to produce masterpieces. Inspired by the earlier ceramists, a handful of Armenian ceramists emerged in the 1970s and onwards, including the Sandrouni brothers (Harout, Garo, and George), Vic Lepejian, and Hagop Antreassian, and established their workshops in the Armenian Quarter. Armenian ceramists transferred the skills to Arab Palestinians.

A piece by Garo Sandrouni, Jerusalem 2012. Private collection.

The Ohannessian (Tako paper factory) and the Mardirossian (Silvana chocolate factory) built their empires in Ramallah and were prominent merchants in the latter half of the 20th century. Both factories became household names; Silvana[236] was synonymous with chocolate and Tako with tissues. Both businesses closed around 2002-2003 during the second Palestinian *intifada* (uprising)[237] which took its toll on the Palestinian economy in general.

George Garabedian expanded George's International Tours. His legacy was assumed by his son Garo who expanded the company's operations and founded the Christmas Hotel in Jerusalem, and a tourist bus company operational today. M.G. Ohan Shirts and Pajamas Co., established by Megerditch Gosdigian in the 1940s in Ramallah, grew as its products became available across Palestine and Jordan in high end men's clothing stores. Armenian jewelers and goldsmiths dominated the industry into the 1970s, and they were the key artisans and distributors of gold jewelry throughout the West Bank.

Armenian mechanics were well-established in Mamilla before 1948 and it was common to seek the services of a *mekaniki Armani* (Armenian mechanic), especially during the Mandate years. These mechanics left all their equipment behind in 1948 but several retained their skills and reopened their garages when the Wadi El Joz mechanics center evolved in East Jerusalem.

Kalaydjian the burgulgi (from the word *burghul,* cracked wheat in Arabic) continued to supply *burghul* to buyers in Palestinian cities including Bethlehem, Ramallah and Nablus. Mehran Kalaydjian and his family dominated the cracked wheat market with a large business of over 60 employees from the 1940s to the 1970s. UN trucks were often seen loading cracked wheat for distribution and business boomed to such an extent that Mehran Kalaydjian provided a loan to the Patriarchate to cover delayed salary payments on several occasions.[238]

Several Armenian hairdressers for women relocated from West to East Jerusalem and dominated way into the 1980s, including Levon Sarkissian and Khacho Manougian. The Arsenian relocated and established the Jerusalem Grand Pharmacy on Rashid Street in East Jerusalem, serving the Palestinian community for five decades. Hagop Sivsatian was a general manager of the printing press with the Franciscans between the 1950s and the 1970s. Armenian women, including from Jerusalem, became some of the earliest air hostesses from the region. Anton Sahrigian, Perouz Vartan and Minas Minassian were known for selling quality furniture. Kegham and Arshag Markarian had fashion stores on Salaheddin Street and in the Christian Quarter.

Several Palestine-born or raised Armenians emigrated and became renowned elsewhere. To name a few, Diran Voskeritchian, a famous architect who lived in Jerusalem until 1948, moved to Amman and established his company in 1951 (later renamed Diran and Bitar Consultants). He was the architect of over 700 multi-story buildings, monuments, religious sites, and villas in Jordan, Palestine, and elsewhere. Paul Guiragossian was a painter who moved to Beirut and became the President of the Painters' Association there. He finished his first oil painting in 1948 and began exhibiting his works in Beirut and elsewhere. He became one of the most celebrated artists in Lebanon and eventually, the Arab world. Vahram Mavian left Jerusalem for Cyprus, joined the Melkonian Educational Institute, and later the Gulbenkian Foundation, and became one of the top Armenian poets and writers, and a unique voice in Armenian diaspora literature. Boghos Senabian left Jerusalem for Beirut in 1946 and became a known writer and editor of the literary *Pakine* magazine. Kevork Kevorkian became one of the earliest pilots in the late 1950s and Arshak Tavitian became an aeronautical engineer.

Other renowned Palestine-born Armenians or those who lived in Mandatory Palestine have made significant contributions to the Arab world and beyond. Manoug Manougian and other students from Jerusalem created a suborbital rocket in April 1961 in Beirut (called Cedar 1). It was 1.75 meters long, reaching an altitude of about 1,000 meters, followed by Cedar 2 which reached 2,300 meters. Subsequent rockets rose to a height of about 2,500 meters. Manougian (better known as the father of the Lebanese space program) can rightfully claim to be the first to have launched a rocket in the Middle East and he received a lot of publicity.[239] Hovhannes Donabedian, born in Ramallah, studied architecture and engineering at AUB. He returned to Beirut in 1948, worked on a wide range of projects, and established a successful private practice before moving to the US in the mid-1950s. He was an architect in several prominent firms, hospital complexes, and medical centers. He was also an artist with a passion for drawing the human figure and completed over 400 color collages; he was also a poet. In 2019, a film was released about Hovhannes entitled *The Art and Life of Hovhaness S. Donabedian*.[240]

Avedis K Sanjian[241] was born in Marash, Turkey, but had come to Palestine in 1926 and settled in the Armenian Quarter. He was the first graduate student at Michigan to receive a doctorate in Near Eastern Studies. He began his academic career at Harvard University where he developed the first curriculum of Armenological courses in the US and compiled *A Grammar of Classical Armenian* to enable students to learn Armenian. He wrote 10 books and more than 40 articles in English and Armenian on various Armenological subjects. Haig Khatchadourian, born in 1925 in the Old City of Jerusalem, became a Professor of Philosophy at the University of Wisconsin. He also taught at the AUB, the Melkonian Educational Institute in Nicosia, Cyprus, at the Haigazian College, Beirut, and the University of Southern California. He was a recipient of numerous honors and awards, including Outstanding Educators of America Award, 2,000 Intellectuals of the 20th Century, and 2,000 Outstanding Academics of the 21st century. He published 19 books and at least 94 articles.[242]

He wrote a paperback titled *The Quest for Peace between Israel and the Palestinians* (2000) on the status of Jerusalem in which he stated:

> *"East Jerusalem ought to become part - indeed, the capital - of the Palestinian state... However, recognizing Israel's insistence that East Jerusalem is 'nonnegotiable,' I endorsed in 1970 the 1947 UN General Assembly's resolution to internationalize it. That – and Israel's insistence that Jerusalem is eternally Israeli – remains the Israelis' unshakable position. Nevertheless, it is my hope that Israel may eventually agree to relinquishing East Jerusalem to Palestinian rule, provided that (a) a political and administrative formula can be worked out whereby Jerusalem would remain undivided so that, among other things, the city would remain open to all religions, but (b) also allow East Jerusalem to become the capital of the Palestinian state in the same way that West Jerusalem is Israel's capital.*[243]

Abraham Kankashian, a universally popular *Kaghakatsi* and an inspiring teacher at AUB, produced a collection of short stories called *An Armenian Medley,* a reflection of life in the 20th century. Levon Malikian, born in Jerusalem during WWI, was a pioneer clinical psychologist and the most famous psychologist in Lebanon and the Arab world before emigrating to Canada during the Lebanese civil war.

Several Armenians have made their way into journalism. Aram Belian worked with *Al Anba* and *Al Quds* newspapers in Jerusalem, and later with Israel's Arabic television service. Johnny Zakarian became an editor of a newspaper in Connecticut; Oshin Keshishian an editor of a newspaper in Los Angeles; Ara Kalaydjian an editor of a newspaper in Boston; and Arthur Hagopian was a freelance journalist who also worked with an Australian newspaper. Khatcho Khatchadourian was instrumental in launching an English-language newspaper, *The Daily News,* in Kuwait. He also edited *The Jerusalem Times* and *The Kuwait Times* before his untimely death during the Lebanese civil war.[244] Jirair Tutunjian[245] became the youngest Canadian magazine editor on record at the age of 24 and taught at the University of Toronto. During his tenure as editor for six consumer and trade magazines, he won many international and local awards, reported from 110 countries around the world, and authored several books. Nahabet Melkonian was a writer and a journalist. Ashkhen Demirdjian and Fr. Peter Madros (Mardirosian) of Armenian roots were frequent contributors to *Al Quds* newspaper.

David Terzibashian's brother, Abraham Terian (changed from Terzibashian), is an internationally renowned scholar on Armenian patristic and theological literature, an expert on monasticism in the Holy Land, and the author of several titles on the history of the early church. David's older brother George (Kevork Terian) is an ordained Minister at the Armenian Congregational Church in Dawney, California and an expert in biblical classical Hebrew and Greek.

A few Armenians served in the Jordanian military, police and security establishment, including Kapriel Nalbandian and Joseph Hagopian. Karim Ohan was the minister of internal security for many years. Others included Aprahamian, Garo Basmadjian, and Aram Yaghlian. Dentist Berj Hagopian also served in the Jordanian army.[246]

Armenian Immigration from Palestine Post 1948 with Focus on the Past Few Decades

The Armenian community has always remained united in its efforts to protect its members. The political developments in Palestine post-

1948 affected the Armenians of the Holy Land just like the Arab Palestinians and many refugees left to Jordan, Syria, Lebanon or farther afield in search of jobs and better opportunities. At least 25 of my extended family members left between 1948 and the early 1950s. Some of the more well-to-do with property in West Jerusalem who became destitute in East Jerusalem, opted to immigrate to Amman, the expanding capital of Jordan at that time. Today, Armenian refugees who are still alive live with their children and grandchildren in the United States, Canada, Australia, England, Holland, Hungary, Jordan, and Lebanon.

Several business owners who lost their businesses in 1948 were able to restart in East Jerusalem. However, the city started to lose its business clout when Jordan moved the capital from Jerusalem to Amman, and several Jerusalem businesses, including those of Armenians, were "encouraged" to follow suit. The increasingly difficult political environment and volatile economic situation drove many young Armenians - at first *Kaghakatsis*- to emigrate to the Americas, Europe, Canada, Australia, and the Gulf, and many Armenian families and youth were lost from the community between the 1960s and 1980s. *Vanketsis* began to leave in higher numbers but continued to make up the majority of Jerusalem Armenians. Their descendants today are still the majority in the Holy Land.

The once flourishing community of influential business and factory owners, health professionals, goldsmiths, educators, and others is dwindling in numbers, although the Armenian community in the Holy Land and Jerusalem still exists despite the drastic loss of its members. The school is open, as is the Armenian Church and clubs, and a handful of activists keep the community infrastructure alive. Prominent Armenians abroad continue to fund projects and communication between communities has been established to give news about what is happening in Armenia.

The relatively small Armenian community in the Holy Land has made a considerable contribution locally, regionally, and beyond. It has nurtured hundreds of Armenians who have contributed to the Armenian nation in the Middle East and globally, and whose descendants are actively engaged in Armenian community affairs and the evolution of Armenians in the diaspora.

From the early 1900s and up until the 1980s, more than 50 Armenian families lived in the Ramallah /El Bireh area alone, including the Donabedian, Der Bedrossian, Karamanlian, Mardirossian, Ohannessian, Kuftegian, Shahinian, Gosdigian, Odabashian, Melikian, Momjian, Hagopian, Arakelian, and Shanlikian. Less than a handful still maintain a residence in Ramallah and very few Armenian families are left in Jaffa and Nazareth.

A few years after my maternal grandparents and family left to Al Salt in 1948, my aunt Vartoug and her husband Noubar Koyoumdjian were the first from my maternal family to emigrate from Amman to the US in 1953. Vartoug recalled:

> *"It was difficult leaving everything behind and not knowing what awaits you in a foreign country. We worked very hard after our arrival in the US, had opportunities, and did relatively well. As much as we wished to leave memories behind, those memories somehow found their way back. We were always worried for family members left behind and often felt guilty that we were living in better conditions with opportunities. We did our best to sponsor family members to join us and most did in the 1950s and 1960s... but Jerusalem, Amman and Beirut (for my sisters) were always in our hearts despite the challenges of the time. For my parents, they were their haven from their hellish experiences of the*

Genocide. They were in their second home. Our family always wonders what would have been our fate had their not been a Genocide of the Armenian population or had we not left Jerusalem after 1948... we can only imagine."

My aunts who settled in Ohio. and California often mentioned Armenian friends living in the US who were originally from Jerusalem. Glendale is the "little Armenia' in California where many Armenian families from Jerusalem reside. Most are well connected to each other and keep abreast of news from Jerusalem. Several regularly come back for visits. However, it is very painful that most of those Armenians originally from Palestine are elsewhere. Of over 50 *Kaghakatsi* Armenian families in Jerusalem (with more than a household under one family name), less than 15 remain today.[247] Of over 200 families once living in the Convent, some 30 families exist today, including the Nakashian, Kalaydjian, Guiragossian, Bedrossian, Karaguzian, Kahkejian, Aghazarian, Bekarian, Hagopian, Gejekoushian, Kopoushian, Hindoian, and Balian families.[248]

Over one hundred of my extended family members have emigrated since 1948, the majority between 1948 and 1975, and less than a handful remain in Jerusalem. This applies to other Armenian families. It is said that the number of Armenian *Kaghakatsis* living in Sydney were more in number than in Jerusalem. Maybe that was an exaggeration but today the streets of the Armenian Quarter no longer echo with the laughter of *Kaghakatsi* students strolling to *Tarkmanchats* School or other Arab schools in the city, the smell of food from houses of Armenian families crammed in rooms, or the sounds of men and women walking to work. There is little Armenian pedestrian traffic in the Quarter. The JABU hall is near abandoned.[249] While travelling throughout the past four decades, I have visited several of my extended family members living abroad and most are grateful for how their life has evolved, but I have yet to come across one who has not questioned how their life might have been had they stayed in Palestine after 1948 or 1967.

Despite Everything, We Are Still Here

The Armenian Quarter with its dwindling numbers may reflect the history of Armenians in the Holy Land and Jerusalem. Indeed, Palestinians today are concerned more than ever that the Christian population, including Armenians, in the Old City and its immediate environs is approaching the point of no return.[250] Today, all Palestinian Christians and Muslims live under occupation and Israeli policies are a key push factor of Palestinian emigration. In the words of a Palestinian-Armenian human rights defender:

> *"Here in the West Bank, there is no real difference between an Armenian and a Palestinian. Just because I'm Armenian doesn't mean that I'm treated differently from other Palestinians. I am a Palestinian of Armenian descent. We suffer the same harassment that Palestinians suffer and inhale the same tear gas. I grew up witnessing human rights abuses and violence in the West Bank."[251]*

In light of limited expansion and growth, a further decline in numbers seems inevitable. Amid mounting uncertainties, Christian Palestinians, including Armenians, will continue to leave. For the Old City of Jerusalem, Christian efforts at steadfastness will comprise a few hundred people who maintain the holy shrines without a vibrant community of the faithful.

There are still around 1200-1800 Armenians in Jerusalem (in the Armenian Quarter, around the Convent, in East and West Jerusalem, and in the Bethlehem area), and few thousand in Jaffa and Haifa. It is also certain that no matter how big or small the Armenian community is in the Holy Land, Armenian institutions with their invaluable possessions will stay: the churches, the Armenian Patriarchate of Jerusalem, and the museum, and will continue to reflect the rich Armenian history and contribution in the Holy Land. The British Mandate expired, Israelian and Gurney have long passed away, but the Patriarchate as reflected in Sir Henry Gurney's diary remains with its room filled with portraits, the stone staircase, and the *kawasses.* The dedication of the Armenian diaspora in supporting the steadfastness of the Armenian community in the Holy Land cannot be underestimated and must be encouraged as it may be decisive in supporting the community and enabling institutions to develop and prosper.

Several Armenian families remain steadfast in this land of conflict. Albert Aghazarian always identified himself as an Armenian Palestinian. At the commemoration of 70 years of the Palestinian 1948 *Nakba,* he stated:

> *"Despite the painful turbulence the Palestinian people have experienced, we are still here. Be it defeat or victory, this comes from within: it is a state of mind. What matters is that I have not lost hope, and I will continue to be hopeful for as long as we do not accept to switch roles with the Zionists. The ultimate defeat is when we, the oppressed, adopt the role of the oppressor. Our cause is just, and we should never accept the doctrine of the aggressor... The Palestinian people have endured a lot because of the Nakba.*

> *"Any Nakba, catastrophe, does not just happen by accident. It has specific components and requirements. Most importantly, it is based on the*

consideration of other people as less human than you are, that conscientious laws do not apply to them. Unavoidably, this requires you to constantly be reminded that you are facing danger......More words to accentuate the problem we face here are ignorance, greed, and blind hatred. "[252]

Yeghisheh Derderian ended his 1948 diary with:

"The Holy See with its flock is welcoming the year 1949 covered with wounds after 13 months of war with a community economically devastated. In these days, they lay their hope in their Lord. They hope that they will survive to see the Holy Land in peace and prosperity." Unfortunately, that day has not yet materialized and Palestinian suffering continues 75 years after the turning point of 1948. The yearned-for peace will hopefully come to pass for the Armenian Palestinians who have opted to stay in Palestine-Israel.

I often remember my father asking me - and more so as he got older and into his late nineties - on almost a daily base, when peace would come to this area. The night before he passed away in 2020, and while he was half asleep, he spoke of moving incessantly throughout his life. He remembered his childhood years carrying vegetables from Battir (a village in Bethlehem) to Jerusalem to feed his family during the strikes of 1936, his school years in West Jerusalem, the band he was part of and the parties at the *Parisiradz* in the Armenian club, the power struggles among clergy in the Armenian Patriarchate of Jerusalem, the accommodation of Armenians in the Armenian Convent and the Armenian Quarter in 1948, and more. He told us of his long history in this country. This record of historical events was very much the testimony of a resilient Armenian Palestinian deep rooted in the history of his country, and proud to have contributed to his country and people. These were his last words, not knowing to whom he was speaking to while we listened attentively. He passed away after a full life in which he had witnessed joy and sorrow, loss of land, ongoing conflict and still no peace in his lifetime. He had lived and witnessed firsthand the 1936 uprising, the events of 1948, the 1967 War, the first and second Palestinian *intifadas,* and a belligerent occupation with ongoing conflict. Unfortunately, he did not experience the peace he yearned for and hoped would one day materialize with the injustices and wrongdoings that befell Palestinians rectified. It did not happen in his lifetime.[253]

Conclusion

This book has focused on a period of modern history to provide an understanding of the contemporary status of Armenians, primarily in the Holy Land.

To understand the Armenian presence today in Palestine-Israel, you need to be aware of their uninterrupted presence in the Holy Land for 1700 years, and their key contribution to social, religious, and cultural life in which Armenian ethnic, cultural, and religious characteristics were preserved despite all odds.

In modern history, it is imperative to illuminate the status of the Armenian community throughout the Mandate period, culminating in 1948 and the aftermath with the 1967 War and occupation of the rest of Palestine. The subsequent political developments continue to have an impact on the Armenian presence in Palestine.

This book is a humble attempt to reflect through an Armenian eye on Armenian life during the years of the British Mandate over Palestine, a turbulent historical period culminating in the *Nakba*. It is also a hopeful attempt to save a rich and historic Armenian community challenged by the politics of the region. It is great to be proud of the Armenian presence in the Holy Land in one-sixth of the Old City of Jerusalem, but it is of equal or more important to preserve what you have, to understand the plight of Armenians, and enable them to continue their presence and witness in the Holy Land, especially in Jerusalem. Armenians of the Holy Land and Jerusalem are an important part of the City's mosaic to be nurtured and preserved. Their continued presence and witness in the Holy Land is imperative but this is contingent upon peace and stability, both currently absent but these could become reality with a genuine will for peace and prosperity for all.

Annex 1.
Shelling of the Armenian Quarter (not exhaustive)[254]

Date	Affected site	Damage /loss /action taken
Jan 7	Bomb exploded at Jaffa Gate.	56 wounded, 15 died, including two Armenians.
May 15	The Convent closed its doors by order of the police station in the Old City.	A bloody day in the Old City. The Citadel began to roar and the Patriarchate kitchen had to feed over 3500 people.
May 16	A bomb fell on St. James Street and several smaller bombs after mass at the Cathedral. Several shells fell in the afternoon from the Jewish Quarter in the Old City and from Jewish neighborhoods outside the city walls. They fell in the gardens of the Patriarchate, the seminary building, on the school and on the Holy Archangels Convent. Bombs in the evening: three flying bombs fell in the seminary, two of which did not explode.	Bombs shook the St. James Cathedral. Several wounded and, for the first time, a long line of stretchers had to be rushed to the newly established hospital at the Austrian Hospice near the Via Dolorosa. The Armenian Quarter had electricity and water cut off and all phone lines were disrupted. The Armenian Quarter was cut off from the Old City and New City. The first casualties were received in the Convent infirmary. The Patriarch personally appealed to the city authorities, to UN representatives and foreign consuls, and to representatives of the Red Cross, with no results. Those sheltering in the school were transferred to the Holy St. Etchmiadzin Chapel and to the gallery of the Cathedral for safety. Sandbags were placed at all vulnerable points in the Convent. All church services in the Cathedral were suspended. Two bombs were diffused by Elia Bedrossian.

May 18	Bomb fell in the courtyard of the priests' new quarters. In the evening a bomb fell on the forecourt of St. James Cathedral.	The infirmary was full of 32 injured people in the morning and 12 in the evening, with three dead bodies. The injured had shrapnel in their bodies. The wounded received first aid and shrapnel was removed from the injured before sending them to hospital for surgery. This marked the first day of tears for the 3500 residents of the Convent and many families had one of their members affected.
May 19	Bomb fell on the large court of the monastery.	The wounded moved to the infirmary and received immediate medical treatment.
May 20	Big bomb fell on the roof top of St. Echmiadzin near the belfry. Bombs fell on residential quarters and a bomb fell near the seminary and near the Church of Holy Archangels.	Bomb tore four meters square off the edge of the roof and its iron grill heavily damaged the structure of the belfry. Several residential rooms were damaged and one of the bombs was safely dismantled by Elia Bedrossian.
May 21-24	Shelling continued with short pauses. Bombs fell in front of the Gulbenkian library, in front of the main gate of the monastery, and on the Kalaydjian wheat factory.	Front façade, the right wing and windows of the library were smashed. Doors of four shops and the pavement in front of the main gate were destroyed and a fire started at the wheat factory. The wounded were treated at infirmary.
May 25	Three big bombs fell in the courtyard.	Several injuries and deaths.
May 26	Bombs fell in the Patriarchate garden behind the library.	Walls and windows damaged and several injured.

May 27	Eight injured in the evening.	
July 10	After a one-month truce, a big bomb fell in the morning on one of the roofs of the Convent.	Three kitchens were destroyed, two women seriously wounded and five men were wounded by shrapnel.
July 11	Big bomb fell on St. Saviour monastery and the priests' old quarters.	Considerable damage to the surroundings.
July 13-14	Continuous shooting and shelling.	A building belonging to the Greek Patriarchate just outside Jaffa Gate was blown up.
July 15	15 bombs fell in the courtyard of the Gulbenkian library and St. James Street.	Large craters were caused.
July 16	Seven hours of continuous shelling in the Old City from the Jewish side of the city. Of 500 shells, 100 fell on the Armenian Quarter.	Big mortars penetrated roof tops and destroyed doors, and damaged water tanks and walls. Miraculously, only a few were wounded and were treated in the infirmary.
1st week in Sept	Fighting was concentrated around Jaffa Gate, Zion Gate and Damascus Gate.	Heightened anxiety and danger due to the proximity of the Armenian Quarter to Jaffa and Zion Gates.
Sept 11	Intense shelling the whole night of the façade of Zion Gate and many shells in the Old City.	

Sept 12	Fighting around Jaffa Gate. Two mortars fell inside the gate at 5 am. At 6:30 a big mortar fell at the main gate of the Convent. In the evening, another shell fell in the monastery courtyard.	Many wounded (24). The gate area looked like a slaughterhouse. Three women killed and several wounded. The injured were treated at the infirmary with some rushed to the hospital.
Sept 13-16	Shelling at night directed at the Old City Gates.	
Sept 24-25	Several mortars fell on the Holy Archangels Convent.	
Nov 1948	Ongoing shelling.	

Endnotes

1. Local Armenians whose roots in the Holy Land go back hundreds of years.

2. My grandparents (grandfather aged 13 and grandmother aged 9) survived the liquidation and deportation of Armenians from Ottoman Turkey between 1878 and 1923. More than 1.5 million Armenians were killed in 1915 in what is known as the Armenian Genocide. It is estimated that half a million Armenians outside of the borders of the present State of Armenia survived the mass murder.

3. It was thought that the Genocide survivors - mostly orphans – would be short-term visitors who would return to their original homes. They were also known as *Vanketsis* (living in the Convent) as most of them were accommodated in the Armenian Convent (*vank* in Armenian).

4. The *Nakba* of 1948 refers to the mass expulsion of Palestinian Arabs from British Mandate Palestine between 1947 and 1949 during the creation of the State of Israel. Between 750,000 -950,000 of the indigenous 1,400,000 Palestinians became refugees, either internally displaced or in the diaspora. Their properties were seized and transferred to the State of Israel for the use of the Jewish people. Over 500 Palestinian villages were demolished. The *Nakba* started with intermittent violent attacks in 1946, intensifying in November 1947, and an Armistice Agreement reached in 1948. Most Israeli historians claim that it was a voluntary exodus by Palestinians rather than expulsion, and that few massacres occurred. This has been contested throughout the years, with more vocal Israeli historians and others referring to forced expulsion and accompanying violence and atrocities: see Ephraim Karsh, Shabtai Teveth, Simha Flapan, Benny Morris, Ilan Pappe, and Norman Finkelstein. Their accounts have been aided by the relative opening of the Israeli archives which have exposed historical fabrications. Salman Abu Sitta puts the number of demolished Palestinian villages at 530, Walid Al-Khalidi at 418, and Benny Morris at 369 (See Salman Abu Sittah (2011). Palestine Atlas. Palestine Land Society. London p.106).

5. In 1988 the Palestine National Council, which represents all Palestinians in Palestine and the diaspora, recognized the State of Israel on 78% of historic Palestine, and declared a State of Palestine on the remaining 22%, which included land occupied by Israel in the 1967 Arab-Israeli War. In 2012, Palestine pursued an upgrade in status from "observer entity" to "non-member observer state" at the UN. On 29 November 2012, General Assembly Resolution 67/19 passed by a vote of 138-9 (41 abstaining). Palestine was

upgraded to "non-member observer state" status in the United Nations, like that of the <u>Holy See</u>. The change in status is *de facto* recognition of the sovereign state of Palestine.

6. After WWI, Great Britain assumed a Mandate for Palestine with Jerusalem as its administrative center. Jaffa has fallen into the hands of the British in November 1917, and Jerusalem in December 1917. Palestine was under military rule for two and a half years until the British instituted a civilian government in June 1920. The Palestine Mandate was established by the League of Nations in 1922 and was entrusted to Britain as the ruling authority. In April 1947 the British declared their intention to end their Mandate over Palestine. In November 1947, the UN recommended the division of Palestine with Jerusalem as a *corpus separatum* under a special international regime administered by the UN (A/RES/181 of November 29,1947). On 15 May 1948, the British left and violence erupted. The Jewish population, then less than 10% in Palestine, established statehood over 50% of the territory, dividing Jerusalem and gaining momentum at the UN. The newly established State of Israel ended up with 77% of the total territory, including West Jerusalem, while 750,000-950,000 Palestinians became refugees in the diaspora or displaced internally.

7. For example: Varsen Aghabekian (2021*). A Palestinian Armenian: The Intertwine between the Social and the Political.* The book documents the recent history of Palestinian Armenians, particularly in Jerusalem, and celebrates their achievements despite the dire political and economic challenges of a volatile environment. Father Koryoun Baghdasarian (2019, 2021), *The Secrets of the Armenian Quarter of Jerusalem,* and Der Matossian (2011 and 2018) described the conditions of Armenians in Palestine during the British Mandate. See also Garo Sandrouni (2000) on Armenians in Jerusalem; Jacob Orfali (Hagop Khatcherian) (1987); Elia Kahvedjian (1995) *From the Red Desert to Jerusalem-* the second half of the book is an almost sociological report on Armenian Jerusalem through several wars from the mid-1920s to the early 1990s; and John Melkon Rose (1993) on living as an Armenian in Jerusalem during the British Mandate and afterwards. Rose was one of the few non-Jews who remained in West Jerusalem until 1952 when he relocated to East Jerusalem.

George/Kevork Hintlian (both names used interchangeably in this book) wrote various works from 1976 and onwards on the history of the Armenians in the Holy Land and describing life in Jerusalem based on his collection of oral histories over decades. Also, Victor Azaria (1984), Assadour Antreassian (1969), Harutune Mushian (1952), Jirair Tutunjian, Professor Avedis Sanjian, Arthur Hagopian, Ara Sanjian, Harry Hagopian, Harut Sassounian, Anoush Nakashian, Albert Aghazarian and his daughters Elise and Arda have all reflected on the lives of Armenians in the Holy Land.

The life of Armenians during the 1948 war was also covered in the Armenian Patriarchate of Jerusalem's on/off monthly *Sion* magazine which focused on religious, theological, and philosophical issues. Apart from this brief period, Armenians never had a journal that documented the community's political, social, economic, and cultural history and life in Jerusalem and Palestine.

8.   Zachary J. Foster (2011). *Arab Historiography in Mandatory Palestine 1920-1948*. A thesis submitted to the Faculty of the Graduate School of Arts and Sciences of Georgetown University in partial fulfillment of the requirements for the degree of Master of Arts Studies. The appendix to the thesis lists 160 historical books written by Arabs in the land that became British Mandatory Palestine and categorized by city/local histories, Arab history, Palestine histories, regional histories, Islamic, biography, and minority groups, including just one title dedicated to the "minority" group of the Samaritans.

Several Palestinians and Arabs have written on the history of and life in Palestine, the Ottoman period, the Mandate period and the *Nakba*. These authors include Wadi Al Bustani,Tarif Al Khalidi, George Antonious, Khalil Al Sakakini, Mohammed Izzat Darwazeh, Akram Zuaiter, Aref Al-Aref, Hajj Amin Al-Husseini, Fawzi Kaoukji, Musa Al Alami, Mohammed Tarek El-Ifriqi, Emile Al-Ghouri, Khalil Al-Budeiri, Izzat Tannous, Abdulhamid Al Sayeh, Awni Abdulhadi, Bahjat Abu Gharbieh, Hussein Fakhri Al-Khaldi, Rashid El-Hajj Ibrahim, Ahmad Shuqeiri,Walid Al Khalidi, Rashid Al Khalidi, and Anis Al Sayegh.

9.   Bedross Der Matossian (2011). *The Armenians of Palestine 1918-48*. Faculty Publications, Department of History. 121. https://digitalcommons. unl.edu/historyfacpub/121. Accessed January 11, 2021.

10.   The seeds for violence were set earlier with the signing of the Sykes-Picot agreement on May 19, 1916, whereby representatives of Great Britain and France secretly reached an accord to divide most of the Arab land under the rule of the Ottoman Empire into British and French spheres of influence at the end of WWI. This was followed by the Balfour Declaration issued by the British government in 1917 announcing its support for the establishment of a "national home for the Jewish people" in Palestine. At that time, the area was still under the rule of the Ottomans with a majority Arab and a small minority Jewish population.

11.   Part of numerous discussions and notes during 2015-2019 with my father Ohannes (John) Aghabekian, born 1923 and who passed away in 2020.

12.   The Holy Land is used to denote the area of Palestine and is the Christian term for the region. Its boundaries roughly include Israel and the State of Palestine (occupied Palestinian Territory) today.

13.   Including Jerusalem, security, borders and settlements, refugees, water and political prisoners.

14.   Emilio Bonfglio and Johannes Preiser-Kapeller, (2020). *From Ararat to Mount Zion: Armenian Pilgrimage and Presence in the Holy Land, Fourth to Seventh Century*. https://books.ub.uni-heidelberg.de/propylaeum/reader/download/711/711-30-89517-1-10-20200702.pdf

15.   An Armenian officer of the Roman XII legion.

16.   It has a mosaic 6.30 by 3.90 meters in size featuring forty medallions that depict animals and flowers. The Armenian inscription reads: "To the memory, and for the salvation, of all those Armenians whose names are known to the LORD." The mosaic was made between 550 and 580. It was recently moved from its original place to the old seminary in the Convent, which has been rehabilitated as a museum and opened in October 2022.

17.   Some note the formation of the Patriarchate in 1311.

18.   Before becoming Patriarch, Abraham traveled to Mecca to seek protection from Emir Ali against Bedouin raids and to ensure the proprietary rights of the Armenian Church in the Holy Land. He returned with a decree from Prophet Mohammad. An old copy of the decree exists in the Armenian Jerusalem Patriarchate's Mardigian Museum. When Caliph Omar Ibn al-Khattab (634-644) conquered Jerusalem in 638, he installed Abraham as Patriarch of the Armenians. Abraham also became the leader of the Eastern Churches (Assyrians, Copts, Ethiopians, and Jacobites).

19.   There are conflicting figures, but the number 97 appears on the website of the Armenian Patriarchate of Jerusalem.

20.   By the Sultan Abdulmejid I. It preserved the possession and division of Christian holy sites in Jerusalem and Bethlehem and forbade any changes to the status of these sites. This is respected to date.

21.   Rev. Fr. Pakrad Bourjekian (2013). *The Mamluk Inscription of the St. James Armenian Monastery Inside the Armenian Quarter of the Old City, Jerusalem*. Journal of the Society for Armenian Studies, pp.239-251. Al Jaqmaq is also known as ibn 'Abd-Allah al- 'Alā'ī al-Ẓāhiri, the Sultan al-Malik Sayf al-Dīn Abū-Saīd, and belonged to the Burjī Mamluk dynasty; he ruled Egypt, Syria and Palestine between 1438 and 1453, and was of Circassian origin. The edict came as a result of harassment of the St. James Brotherhood of Jerusalem in 1450 by the Treasury Minister. He imposed unprecedented taxes on the Armenian Monastery, prompting the Armenian monks to complain. The Sultan ordered the cancellation of the unprecedented taxes and cursed those imposing taxes or inflicting injustice upon the Armenian Monastery.

22. British-Armenian businessman and philanthropist Calouste Gulbenkian (1869-1955), also known as Mr. Five Per Cent. Gulbenkian played a major role in making the petroleum reserves of the Middle East available to Western development and was the first to exploit Iraqi oil. The Gulbenkian Foundation has its headquarters in Lisbon and has capital of several billions for the advancement of art and education globally.

23. Information from Jirair Tutunjian (personal notes and documents provided by Tutunjian to the author in 2022). Tutunjian was born in Jerusalem and has been a journalist since 1968. At the age of 24, he became the youngest Canadian magazine editor on record and taught at the University of Toronto. During his tenure as editor for six consumer and trade magazines, he won many international and local awards, reported from 110 countries around the world, and authored several books. He has written extensively on Jerusalem and other areas in the Armenian *Keghart* publication in Canada.

24. Jerusalem-born Sydney resident Arthur Hagopian launched the *Kaghakatsi* Family Tree Project to collect genealogical details about the *Kaghakatsis* in the Holy Land.

25. Jirair Tutunjian, *Ancient Armenian Community Faces Oblivion*, and part of his personal notes given to me in 2022.

26. Tania Manougian (2007). The Armenian Community in the Holy Land. *This Week in Palestine* of 30 July 2007.

27. The census of 1922 showed a total population of 752,048, including 589,177 Muslims, 83,790 Jews, 71,464 Christians, and 7,617 "others" (most of them Druze, with about 350 Baha'is and 180 Samaritans). The corresponding percentage breakdown was 87% Christian and Muslim Arab, and 11% Jewish. Bedouins were not counted in the census but a 1930 British study estimated their number to be 70,860. Janet Abu-Lughod. The Demographic War for Palestine. Americans for Middle East Understanding.

28. Bernard Sabella (May 20, 2020). Palestinian Christians Centennial Historical & Demographic Developments. Jerusalem.

29. Laury Haytayan (2011). *Armenian Christians in Jerusalem: 1700 Years of Peaceful Presence*. Politics and Religion. No 2/2011. Vol. V. pp 179-195.

30. Benny Morris (1999). *Righteous Victims*. Vintage Books, New York, p. 83. The Ottomans left Palestine in 1918 after their defeat in the Battle of Megiddo. The British forces entered Palestine in 1917.

31. Salman Abu Sittah (2011), p 21.

32. Bedross Der Matossian (2021). *Armenian Community of Jerusalem: Surviving Against all Odds*. CORNERSTONE. Issue 83, Summer (2021). Published by Sabeel Ecumenical Liberation Theology Center.

33. Bedross Der Matossian. (2011). Op. cit. Also, *The Armenians of Jerusalem in the Modern Period: The Rise and Decline of a Community* (2018). Routledge Handbook on Jerusalem.

34. http://hyeforum.com/index.php?showtopic=32683.

35. Abel Shifferaw. How Armenian Genocide Survivors Sparked a Revolution in Ethiopian Music. https://www.okayafrica.com/documentary-armenian-modern-ethiopian-music/.

36. Letter from Africa: Ethiopia's lost Armenian community. (2 March 2020). https://www.bbc.com/news/world-africa-51672965.

37. Jacob Orfali (Hagop Khatcherian) (1987). *An Armenian from Jerusalem.* Berkeley, CA: Ronin Publishing Inc.

38. Referred to by Saleh Nasser Eddin. He states that Yousef Ibrahim Yazbek spoke of the heroic fight by Armenians on the side of General Allenby against the Turks led by Jamal Pasha. (In the book *Armenians: A People and a Cause,* 1988, First Edition. Published by Dar Al Taqaddumieh Publishing, Lebanon, in Arabic.)

39. Bedros Der Matossian sian (2011). Op. cit. (refering to Manoogians' *Hay Yerusaghem*).

40. Ironically, Mandatory Palestine witnessed the atrocities of the *Nakba* some years later.

41. For example, in some interviews with Golda Meir (1889-1978), the fourth Prime Minster of Israel (1969-1974), she stated that she was a Palestinian from 1921-1948 and carried a Palestinian passport. In other interviews, she stated that there was no such thing as Palestinians.

42. Bedross Der Matossian (2011).

43. From an interview with Kevork /George Hintlian with whom I held numerous discussions throughout 2020-2022. Hintlian is a historian and archivist in the Armenian Patriarchate who eloquently described the intertwine between history and politics of the Armenians in the Holy Land. Hintlian succeeded his father Garbis Hintlian, a survivor of the Armenian Genocide who served five Patriarchs in the Armenian Patriarchate as the Secretary of Property for 55 years from 1926 to 1981. In 1971 George was recruited while teaching at Bir Zeit College to succeed his father at the Patriarchate and to assume broader authority as the archivist, public relations officer, and spokesman. Between Hintlian the father and the son, there is some 75 years of service and memories of work for the Armenian Patriarchate of Jerusalem.

44. In a diary by Father Yeghishe Derderian (later to become Armenian Patriarch of Jerusalem 1960-1990). Published in the Almanac of the Armenian

Patriarchate of Jerusalem covering the period from November 1947 to December 1948, and printed in January 1949. This diary is one of the few detailed diaries of the 1948 War in Jerusalem. Although it specifically refers to events in the Armenian Quarter, it provides information on conditions in the city during the period from November 1947 to December 1948.

45. Anush Babajanyan (January 5, 2018). https://eurasianet.org/Armenia-community-in-jerusalem-shrinks-but-preserves. Accessed January 11, 2021.

46. From interviews with Hintlian in Jerusalem, 2020-2023.

47. In Yeghishe Derderian's diary.

48. An unpublished paper in Arabic titled *The Arab Christian Palestinians in Gaza: I Was With Them* lists 13 people of Armenian origin among the 1300 Christians remaining in Gaza in 2015. It lists them under the family names Missak, Artin and Abagian. (2015).

49. Mentioned in Seth J. Frantzman (thesis 2006). *Identity and Inclination: The Arab Christians Between Zionism and Islam.* Hebrew University.

50. Harry Hagopian. The Armenian Church in the Holy Land. http://Armenian-jerusalem.org

51. Ara Sanjian. (2003). *The Armenian Church and Community in Jerusalem.* In Anthony Mahoney (ed.). The Christian Communities of Jerusalem and the Holy Land: Studies in History, Religion and Politics. Cardiff: University of Wales Press.

52. Bedross Der Matossian (2021).

53. Interview with Berj Gegekoushian in Jerusalem, 2022.

54. A Palestinian village 6.4 km west of Bethlehem and to the southwest of Jerusalem. In Ottoman and British Mandate times, it was part of a strip of small villages linked to Jerusalem. Battir is on 2014 List of World Heritage in Danger.

55. Discussions with Ohannes Aghabekian in Jerusalem over several years.

56. During a discussion with Chris Aghabekian in the US in 1998.

57. Discussions with Ohannes Aghabekian in Jerusalem.

58. The sisters Margret, born 1889, and Takouhi (Malakeh), born 1891, trained as nurses in the 1910s in Hebron Hospital. They became fluent in English and German alongside Arabic and Armenian. They both studied nursing at the Syrian Protestant College of Beirut (renamed the American University of Beirut in 1920), and worked in Aleppo where they were the only two female nurses in the 50-bed hospital. They also worked in Beirut and Egypt for a short time before returning to Palestine. Malakeh later qualified as

a midwife at Berlin University Department of Midwifery in 1919 and returned to Palestine where she worked at numerous health centers. (See John Melkon Rose (1993). Armenians of Jerusalem: Memories of Life in Palestine. New York. Radcliffe Press).

59.   Located in the Muslim Quarter about 400 meters from the Al-Aqsa Mosque compound, next to the *Zawiya Al Naqshabandiyya*. It is situated close to the Via Dolorosa on the site of the third and fourth Stations of the Cross in the Old City of Jerusalem.

60.   Sossie Andézian (2017). A New Ethno-Religious Entity in British Mandate Palestine: The Armenian Catholic Community. journals.openedition.org. https://doi.org/10.4000/eac.1117. Accessed February 16, 2021.

61.   From a note from Jirair Tutunjian, 2022.

62.   See Sylva Natalie Manoogian (2013). The Calouste Gulbenkian Library, *Armenian Patriarchate of Jerusalem, 1925-1990: An Historical Portrait of a Monastic and Lay Community*. Intellectual Resource Center. A dissertation submitted in partial satisfaction of the requirements for the degree Doctor of Philosophy in Library and Information Science. University of California LA.

63.   The Gulbenkian Foundation has largely paid for the renovation works to the seminary and maintained the physical structure and operation of the Gulbenkian library. The library is considered one of the most important in the Armenian diaspora. It houses a rich collection of books and periodicals dating back to the early 19th century and is open to all. When Calouste Gulbenkian died in 1955, he bequeathed a sum of money as continuous support for the library. See Astrig Tchamkerten (2006). *The Gulbenkians in Jerusalem*. Calouste Gulbenkian Foundation. Lisbon.

64.   Interviews with Berj Gegekoushian and Varouj Ishkhanian in Jerusalem, 2022, and confirmed in notes provided to the author by Jirair Tutunjian.

65.   Mamilla neighborhood was established in the late 19th century outside the Old City to the west of Jaffa Gate. It was a mixed Jewish-Arab business district up until 1948.

66.   The Irgun, led by Menachem Begin (later Prime Minister of Israel 1977-1983) and the Stern Gang, a dissident of the Irgun led by Avraham Stern.

67.   John Melkon Rose (1993). Also, from interviews with George Hintlian 2020-2022.

68.   Bedross Der Matossian (2011).

69.   Vartouhi Kukeyan was born in Jerusalem in the late 1950s. She was a graduate of the Armenian school and then of the AVH School of Nursing in the late 1970s. She received a master's degree from the US. She was one

of the best-known teachers of midwifery in several Palestinian educational programs during the 1990s and gained the title "the mother of modern midwifery in Palestine." She lives in the Armenian Quarter in the Old City of Jerusalem.

70. Information from Serop Sahagian, Jerusalem, 2022.

71. Information from Marie Ohannessian, 2022.

72. Information from Garo Gosdigian, 2021.

73. Bedross Der Matossian (2021).

74. Harry Hagopian (2002).

75. Varsen Aghabekian (2021).

76. *Hoyetchmen's* 50th anniversary report (1937-1987). Jerusalem.

77. For Palestinian Armenian personalities in various fields, mostly born in the first half of the 20th century, see Varsen Aghabekian (2021).

78. The school was built in 1926 by the Società di San Paolo of Milan and designed by the Italian architect Antonio Berluzzi, who designed many buildings in Jerusalem during this period. It was opened initially in the 1920s as a school and then turned into a college in the 1930s. It closed in 1947 when the area around it was declared a security zone. The school served Christians, Arabs, and Jews.

79. See Zachary J. Foster (2011).

80. Information from Kevork Hintlian in interviews in Jerusalem from 2020 to 2022.

81. Information obtained from Yvonne and Michael Zakarian in 2021. Both are my paternal second cousins who grew up in the Armenian Quarter. Yvonne is Michael's youngest sister. Her father was shot by a sniper's bullet in 1948 when Yvonne was still in her mother's womb. After graduation from the Armenian school in Jerusalem, Yvonne travelled to Holland and still lives there. Her older brother Michael went to the US for higher studies in the 1960s, then returned to Jerusalem and married Armenian Jerusalemite Maro Kahvedjian, then spent a few more years in the US. He has been back in Jerusalem for over two decades now and lives in the house where his uncle Paul Zakarian and the Gazmararians once lived.

82. John Melkon Rose (1993).

83. Interview with Ohannes Aghabekian in Jerusalem

84. https://www.nevo.co.il/law_html/law21/pg-e-0562-2.pdf. Urban property tax ordinances, 1928-1935. Order No.7 of 1936, by the High Commissioner.

85.   Interview with Michael Genevisian in Jerusalem in 2022. Genevisian is a tour guide who was born in 1940, raised in the Armenian Quarter, and still lives there today.

86.   Information from Vartouhi Kukeyan and Hoppig Marashlian from interviews in Jerusalem in 2022. Hoppig Marashlian is my paternal second cousin. She was born in the Armenian Quarter and continues to live in the same house in which she was born 65 years ago, and the same house in which her grandfather resided over 100 years ago adjoining the Jewish Quarter. A self-taught chef fluent in four languages.

87.   Bedross Der Mattossian, (2011) and (2018). The Christian religious orders favored accommodation with the ruling authority. Thus, the Mandate authority granted the religious hierarchy absolute authority with minimal representation in governance by the laity.

88.   Several visionary Patriarchs bought prime land and/or properties for investment and as a source of regular income for the Patriarchate including the land of the monastery of Baron Deir in Bethlehem. (Most of its land today has been confiscated by the Government of Israel in 2003).

89.   Interview with Kevork Hintlian in Jerusalem, 2022

90.   Mordechai Weingarten was the person who announced the surrender of the Jewish Quarter to the Arab Legion. He had four daughters. One of his daughters, came to the Armenian Quarter one month after the 1967 War to check on their house and those of my father, Hortanan's (Jordan Chillingirian) family and other neighbors whom they new before 1948. It was a very short encounter with reminiscenses of the past. Shortly afterwards, she invited the neighbors to one of her children's weddings, but later contact was minimal. In the 1970s,she turned their residence in the Jewish Quarter into a museum..

91.   Interview with Ohannes (John) Aghabekian. By 1955 my father had worked for the British Mandate in Jerusalem, in Cyprus, with Aramco in Saudi Arabia, and with UNRWA. He also worked for a short time with Bir Zeit University and AVH in Jerusalem. He was the last male from the Aghabekian family in Jerusalem in 2020. His death marked the end of the presence of the Aghabekian family in the Holy Land for over 200 years.

92.   Interview with Vartouhi Kukeyan in Jerusalem, 2022.

93.   Interview with Vartouhi Kukeyan in Jerusalem, 2022.

94.   Vincent Lemire (2017). *Jerusalem 1900. The Holy City in the Age of Possibilities*. Chicago University Press. See also Louis Fishman (2018) The Limitations of Citadinate in Late Ottoman Jerusalem https://www.jstor.org/stable/10.1163/j.ctvbqs2zk.37 from the book *Ordinary Jerusalem*

1840-1940: Opening New Archives, Revisiting a Global City by Angelos Dalachanis and Vincent Lemire. Brill Series: Open Jerusalem.

95.   Michelle U. Compos. (2011). *Ottoman Brothers: Muslims, Christians, and Jews in Early Twentieth Century Palestine.* Stanford, California. Stanford University Press. See also Manachem Kline (2014). Lives in Common: Arabs and Jews in Jerusalem, Jaffa, and Hebron. Oxford University Press, and Salim Tamari. (2000). Jerusalem's Ottoman Modernity: The times and Lives of Wasif Jawhariyyeh. In Jerusalem Quarterly.No.9.

96.   Seth J. Frantzman (2006).

97.   From an interview with Ishkhanian in Jerusalem in Jerusalem in 2022. Ishkhanian was an apprentice in the studio of his grandfather, Krikor Ishkhanian, on Jaffa Street. He moved the studio to the Old City's Christian Quarter in 1964 and it remained there until it closed a decade ago. His business included taking passport photos, portraits, weddings, and covering daily life in the city. He produced postcards of old prints taken by his grandfather. Aside from his studio work, he worked as a photographer for *al-Jihad, al-Filastin* and *al-Diffa* newspapers.

98.   See Menachem Klein (2014). *Lives in Common: Arabs and Jews in Jerusalem, Jaffa, and Hebron,* p.105. Hurst and Company. London.

99.   See Salim Tamari (Summer 2014). Issa Al Issa's Unorthodoxy: Banned in Jerusalem, Permitted in Jaffa. In Jerusalem Quarterly, p. 97.

100.   Interview with George Hintlian in Jerusalem, 2022.

101.   See Rochelle Davis. *Growing up Palestinian in Jerusalem before 1948: Childhood Memories of Communal Life, Education, and Political Awareness.* Book chapter in Jerusalem Interrupted: Modernity and Colonial Transformation 1917–Present, edited by Lena Jayyusi, Interlink Publishers 2015, pp.187-210.

102.   https://themedialine.org/life-lines-armenian-ceramists-that-changed-the -face-of-Jerusalem

103.   List by David Terzibashian and provided by Hoppig Marashlian.

104.   Information from George Hintlian, 2021.

105.   Information from Saro Nakashian in Jerusalem, 2021. Nakashian is a prominent figure in higher education in Palestine having taught for over 30 years and is department chair at Bir Zeit University. He is also the head of an organization called Education for Employment serving Palestinian youth. He holds a doctorate in business and lives in East Jerusalem. Arshag was Saro's grandfather.

106.   Information from George Hintlian.

107.   List by David Terzibashian and provided by Hoppig Mareshlian.

108.   Most of the residents in the neighborhood knew Mary and others met her
       during her visits to refugee camps in the Ramallah area. The private letters
       of John Whiting of the American Colony describe elderly people with
       hacking coughs and babies crying, with Mary taking the children to the baby
       clinic. Information from George Hintlian. John Whiting (1882-1951) was a
       key member of the American Colony, a Christian community of Americans,
       Swedes, and others based in Jerusalem.

109.   Garabedian was a priest who moved from Anatolia to become the archivist
       at St James Armenian Church and who was instrumental in teaching several
       apprentices. Garabedian's election as Patriarch (1865-1885) prompted him
       to teach photography to the sons of the city's Armenian community. His
       school produced many of the first local photographers in Palestine and
       the Levant. www.paljourneys.org Palestine Photographers before 1948:
       Palestine Journey. Accessed January 15, 2021.

110.   Keghart (Sept 2014). Book review by Jirair Tutunjian of *From the Red
       Desert to Jerusalem* by Elia Kahvedjian.

111.   The Diaries of Constantine Mavrides, May 15-December 30, 1948.
       Memoranda 1-5. An appendix in *Jerusalem 1948: The Arab
       Neighborhoods and Their Fate in the War*. (2nd edition 2002).
       Salim Tamari (Editor), Institute of Palestine Studies and Badil
       Resource Center, pp.277-293.

112.   Sir Henry was appointed Chief Secretary to Palestine in 1946, serving until
       the end of British rule there in 1948, and he was instrumental in crafting
       British policy during the Jewish insurgency in Palestine. He returned to
       London on May 14 with the expiry of the Mandate. He was then appointed
       High Commissioner of Malaysia, where he was murdered by communist
       insurgents in 1951.

113.   Copy of an excerpt provided by Kevork Hintlian. More on Gurney in Golani,
       Motti, *The End of the British Mandate for Palestine, 1948: The Diary of Sir
       Henry Gurney.* (2009). Palgrave Macmillan.

114.   Maria Chiara Rioli (2020). *Catholic Humanitarian Assistance for Palestinian
       Refugees* in the book Christian Missions and Humanitarianism in the Middle
       East 1850-1950, edited by Inger Okkenhaug and Karene Summerer, pp.253-
       276. Brill. DOI: https://doi.org/10.1163/9789004434530_013

115.   In *Sion* magazine. Issue May-June 1948, p179.

116.   The events of 1948 with injured, deaths, and the destruction of Armenian
       property took its toll on Israelian. He could not be diagnosed in Jerusalem,

and he was taken to Beirut for his "mysterious malady." He underwent unsuccessful exploratory surgery for what was diagnosed as an acute infection of the spinal marrow and passed away a few days after the operation. His sealed casket was transported to Jerusalem via Amman and ceremoniously buried in the courtyard of the main entrance to the Saint James Cathedral because the traditional Patriarchal burial ground outside the walls had been declared "no man's land." See Krikorian, (2009).

117. James Stocker, (2017). *The United States and the Struggle in the Armenian Patriarchate of Jerusalem 1955-1960.* Jerusalem Quarterly 71. https://oldwebsite.palestine-studies.org/jq/issue/71.

118. Interview with Varouj Ishkhanian in Jerusalem, 2022.

119. Interview with Berj Gegekoushian in Jerusalem, 2022.

120. *Sion* magazine November-December1949, pages 324-334.

121. Rev. Hugh Jones, diary of events, May–July 1948. Christ Church, Jerusalem.

122. John Rose (1993).

123. From Yeghishe Derderian's diary.

124. Interview with George Hintlian in Jerusalem, 2021.

125. Interview with Michael Genevisian in Jerusalem, 2022.

126. Interviews with Varouj Ishkhanian and Kevork Hintlian in Jerusalem, 2022. The man serving the food to the queuing children was Ghazaros Kushturian.

127. Interview with Berj Gegekoushian in Jerusalem, 2022.

128. Part of this statement appeared in Varsen Aghabekian (2021). *A Palestinian Armenian: The Intertwine between the Social and the Political.* Dar Al Kalima University Press.

129. An ancient trading city and administrative centre in the center of *Jordan,* 35 km from Amman, and on the old main highway (often called the Salṭ road) leading from Amman to Jerusalem. At that time Amman was still a small village; its status changed when it became the capital of independent Jordan in 1946.

130. Interview with Berj Gegekoushian in Jerusalem, 2022.

131. From Patriarch Yeghishe Derderian's diary.

132. Astrig Tchamkerten (2006). *The Gulbenkians in Jerusalem.* Calouste Gulbenkian Foundation. Lisbon.

133. First row right to left: Krikor Sarkissian, Souren Azazian, Zaven Simonian. Second row: Shousahan Hovsepian, Khatoun Sarkissian, Dr. Krikor

Daghlian, Dr. Puzant Semergian, Vartouhi Mardirossian, Hagop Meneshian. Third row: John Baghsarian, Dikran Bedrossian, Garbis Ohanian, Garabed Chapadarian, Hagop Janoyan, Hovsep Andonian, Ghazaros Kushturian, Hethum Bedevian. Fourth row: Aram Megerdichian, Boghos Emerzian, Sarkis Atikian, Krikor Tutunjian, Levon Daghlian, Garo Nazigian, Kevork Hovsepian. Photo from the Hoyetchmen anniversary book.

134.   From Yeghishe Derderian's diary.

135.   After being a site for rest and relaxation for British Mandate soldiers, AVH became a base for a massive humanitarian response after May 14, 1948, and was converted into a hospital in 1949. It became the largest hospital serving Palestinian refugees. In 1948, there were no hospitals in East Jerusalem while 18 hospitals were in operation in West Jerusalem. It was Count Bernadotte who has ordered the transformation of the AVH into a hospital. See LWF-A Heritage of Service 1948-2010. htpps://Jerusalem.lutheranworld.org

136.   Interview with Lucy Khatcherian Aghabekian in Jerusalem, 2020. Lucy is my mother and a descendent of parents who were Armenian Genocide survivors. She graduated from the AVH School of Nursing in 1955 prior to marrying Ohannes (John) Aghabekian in 1956. She served as a nurse in different capacities in various health centers under the Jordanian rule of the West Bank, and afterwards during the Israeli occupation until she retired in the late 1980s. Aside from living for few years in Jordan, she has lived most of her life in East Jerusalem. She is 88 years old.

137.   The Hospice continued to serve as hospital until the 1980s when it was turned into a guest house. My youngest sister Madlen Aghabekian was born in a room off this corridor in 1964.

138.   From Yeghishe Derderian's diary.

139.   In response to the atrocities of the *Nakba*, other churches and organisations set up shelters and food for those displaced, especially in Jerusalem where there were several initiatives to host and shelter victims such as by Hind Al Husseini and the formation of Dar Al Tifel Al Arabi.

140.   Vartouhi Khatcherian Koyoumdgian was born in 1929 and passed away in Ohio, US in 2014. She married Noubar Kouyoumdgian, also the descendent of a Genocide survivor, who she met in Amman and married in 1953. They emigrated to the US in 1954. I spent most of my undergraduate university years in her home in Hinckley, Ohio.

141.   From Yeghishe Derderian's diary.

142.   Chapter Fourteen: *Destruction and Desecration of Christian Holy Places and Violations of Christian Religious Rights.* In Issa Nakhleh (1991). Encyclopedia of the Palestine Problem. Intercontinental Books. New York.

143. From notes by Jirair Tutunjian.

144. Letter published in *Sion* magazine May-June 1948, page 180

145. Mentioned by most interviewees.

146. Interview with Vartouhi Kukeyan in Jerusalem, 2022.

147. Interview with George Hintlian in Jerusalem, 2021.

148. In his diary, Constantine Mavrides confirms the severity of the shelling, which continued past midnight with around one shell fired every two minutes to make a total of 600 mortar shells fired at targets in the Holy City and causing fires and destruction. See The Diaries of Constantine Mavrides, May 15-December 30, 1948. Memoranda 1-5, pp.284-286. Op.cit.

149. From Yeghishe Derderian's diary.

150. From an interview with George Hintlian in Jerusalem, 2022.

151. From an interview with Michael Zakarian in Jerusalem, 2022.

152. Interview with Vartouhi Kukeyan in Jerusalem, 2022.

153. Interviews with Kevork Hintlian in Jerusalem, 2020 and 2022.

154. *Sion* magazine, (1947 and 1948).

155. Interviews with Kevork Hitlian, Berj Gegekoushian, and Dikran Bakerjian in Jerusalem, 2022.

156. Interview with Kevork Hintlian in Jerusalem, 2021.

157. Interview with Kevork Hintlian in Jerusalem, 2021.

158. Interview with Dikran Bakerjian in Jerusalem,2021. Dikran is my paternal second cousin, born and raised in the Armenian Quarter. A dental technician whose workshop is in the Armenian Quarter, he continues to live in the same house in which he was born and where his grandparents lived over 100 years ago bordering the Jewish Quarter.

159. Information from George Hintlian in Jerusalem, 2020.

160. Interviews with Vartouhi Kukeyan, Berj Gegekoushian, and Kevork Hintlian in Jerusalem, 2020.

161. Information from an interview with Maurice Bannayan over the phone, 2022.

162. From Harout Kahvedjian through Jirair Tutunjian, 2022.

163. Armenian names were often used with an adjective for added identification. *Sab3 El Leil* in Arabic, for example, implies that Hagop Zakarian was very courageous at night, and 'Shash Garbis' indicates that Garbis was cross-eyed.

164. From an interview with Lucy Khacherian Aghabekian in Jerusalem, 2020.

165. From an interview with Vartouhi Kukeyan in Jerusalem, 2022.

166. From an interview with Dikran Bakerjian. In Jerusalem, 2022.

167. Interview with George Hintlian in Jerusalem, 2021.

168. A Lutheran Armenian survivor of the 1894 massacres who came to Palestine from Diyarbakir. He was known for his philanthropic work and service to the Lutheran Church and to Palestinian refugees, especially between 1949 and 1953.

169. Interview with Kevork Hintlian in Jerusalem, 2021 and 2022.

170. A note from Jirair Tutunjian, 2022.

171. Sa'eed Ammouri (2020). Armenians in Jerusalem's History: Armenian Palestinian is How They Define Themselves. From the article Armenian Pages in the *History of Jerusalem* by Nouwayhed al-Hout. Https:raseef22. net/article. "Drank from the same cup" is a common expression in Arabic to reflect the same fate.

172. One of the largest cities in <u>Jordan</u> located 19 km northeast of Amman.

173. A city north of Amman.

174. From an interview with Michael Genevisian in Jerusalem, 2022.

175. Interview with Hovan Bedrossian and George Hintlian in Jerusalem, 2021.

176. Recollection by Hovan Bedrossian as it appears in Varsen Aghabekian, (2021).

177. Harout Kahvedjian is the eldest son of Elia Kahvedjian (The Photo Elia shop in the Christian Quarter in Jerusalem). He told Jirair Tutunjian this information when asked about the losses his family suffered in the 1948 War. He emigrated to Canada just before the 1967 War and translated to English his father's book *From the Red Desert to Jerusalem.* This autobiography of Urfa-born Elia Kahvedjian, who witnessed the Genocide of Armenians as a five-year-old boy, describes his experiences in Turkey and Syria, and his eventual move to Jerusalem and becoming a renowned photographer.

178. Online interview with Maurice Bannayan, 2022.

179. Interview with Abcar Zakarian in Jerusalem, 2022.

180. Sato Moughalian (2019). *Feast of Ashes: The Life and Art of David Ohannessian.* Stanford University Press.

181. List does not include damage caused by bullets to windows, etc.

182. Nora Arsenian Carmi (2021). *We are Still Here.* CORNERSTONE. Issue 83.

183. Bedross Der Matossian. (2021).

184. Katamon is a neighborhood in south Jerusalem known for its Orthodox San Simon Monastery.

185. Baqa'a in south *Jerusalem* was established in the late 19th century after the completion of the Jerusalem railway station. The area attracted wealthy Muslim, Christian, and Armenian families from the Old City who built mansions there in the 1920s.

186. A neighborhood of Jerusalem constructed between 1924 and 1937 on land purchased from the Greek Orthodox Patriarchate by Constantine Salame, a Christian Arab merchant and contractor.

187. Rochelle Davis (1999). *The Growth of Western Communities, 1917-1948.* In Jerusalem 1948: The Arab Neighborhoods and their Fate in the War. Salim Tamari (editor). Institute of Jerusalem Studies and Badil Resource Center, pp. 32-73.

188. Seth J. Frantzman (2006) with references to Ben Arieh.

189. Ibid.

190. Visits to former homes by the original Palestinian owners have taken place since it became possible after the 1967 War or when some owners who left the country assumed other nationalities and were permitted to enter Israel. Most are denied entry to the house itself but look from the outside.

191. Online interview with John Ramian, 2022.

192. Harry Hagopian (2002). *The Armenian Church in the Holy Land.* London. Melisende Publishers.

193. Interview with George Hintlian in Jerusalem, 2022.

194. *This Week in Palestine.* Issue 225.May 2022. Life in Pre-1948 Jerusalem. www.thisweekinpalestine.com

195. A German Protestant orphanage located outside the Old City of Jerusalem that operated from 1860 to 1940. It was a philanthropic institution that offered academic and vocational training to hundreds of orphaned Arab children. Its graduates where known throughout the region for their «orderliness, discipline, and German language.» Training included in trades such as tailoring, shoemaking, engraving, carpentry, metalwork, pottery, painting, printing, farming, and gardening.

196. The Semiramis Hotel was owned by the Lorenzo and Aboussouan family and blown up by the *Haganah.* Most of the occupants were killed. (John Melkon Rose, 1993.)

197. Nancy Kricorian. Pursuing Justice in a Culture of Impunity: Ivan Karakashian of Defense for Children International Palestine, January 22, 2015. https://armenianweekly.com/2015/01/22/karakashian-palestine/

198. Information from Michael Genevisian and Margo Toumayan (one of the daughters).

199. Information from George Hintlian.

200. Information from Rev. Dr. Mitri Raheb and George Hintlian. Many of the book collections left behind by Palestinians ended up in the Israel National Library while many others were destroyed, looted or damaged.

201. Information from George Hintlian.

202. From an interview with Michael Genevisian in Jerusalem, 2022.

203. Located outside Jaffa Gate to the northwest of the Old City wall.

204. Means "father of the bull" in Arabic and also known as Al Thori. The area was developed in the south of the Old City as a residential quarter in the late 19th century by Muslim and Christian Palestinians.

205. Interview with George Hintlian in Jerusalem, 2022.

206. Discussion with Garo Gosdigian in Jerusalem ,2022

207. The Absentee Property Law of 1950 was first promulgated in December 1948 and stated that any Arab not at his/her place of residence on November 5, 1947, would be considered as absent and their property subject to expropriation by the custodian of enemy property (replaced by the custodian of absentee property). These abandoned dwellings and properties were soon filled by Jewish immigrants, soldiers, and those who left the Jewish Quarter of the Old City

208. Interview with George Hintlian in Jerusalem, 2020.

209. Interview with Alice Zakarian in Jerusalem, 2022.

210. Maria Chiara Rioli, (2020). She lists the Palestinian refugee families who stayed at the Casa Nova in Jerusalem in 1949. The Casa Nova became one of the most important church-related institutions carrying out humanitarian aid work in 1948. The list of refugees in the Casa Nova on September 27, 1948, included 250 people from 70 families from the Musrara, Katamon, Talbiyyeh, Romema, Baqa'a, the German Colony, and Beit Hakerem. In 1952, there were 210 people from 58 families still occupying 94 rooms of the Casa Nova.

211. Notes from Jirair Tutunjian.

212. Sato Moughalian (2019, p.242) states that Tavit Ohannessian, his wife

Victoria, and children Fimi and Garo were among the 750,000 Palestinians displaced by the hostilities.

213. Interview with David Terzibashian in 2021 and 2022.

214. Information provided to Jirair Tutunjian by Nikola Romashuk Hairabedian, the grandson of Yeghias's sister, Dikranouhi Hairabedian.

215. Hintlian states that despite the apolitical stance adopted by Armenians in Palestine, Armenians elsewhere in the Middle East were more inclined to join political parties in their host country such as the early leftist parties in Lebanon, Syria, and Iraq. For example, Arsen Guidour and Madoian.

216. From an interview with Ohannes (John) Aghabekian.

217. A former checkpoint between the Israeli and Jordanian sectors of Jerusalem to the north of the Old City along the Green Line. The first checkpoint was set up at the end of the 1948 War in 1949 until August 1952. It was later moved from the Israeli side of the Gate to the Demilitarized Zone and existed until 1967. Clergy, diplomats and United Nations personnel were allowed passage through the Gate. The Jordanians permitted a twice-monthly supply convoy from the Israeli sector to access Jewish property on Mount Scopus, and there was an annual Christmas crossing for Israeli Christians making a pilgrimage to Bethlehem. Like Christian clergy from other denominations, Armenians with permission could cross the Armistice line and attend to the needs of their faithful in Israel.

218. Harry Hagopian (2002) and George Hintlian (1998).

219. Hoyetchmen anniversary book.

220. Interview with Kevork Hintlian in Jerusalem, 2022.

221. Sanjian, Khachadourian, Manougian, Donabedian, and Bedros Balian who had a printing house but moved to Armenia after 1948. Philip Derderian had a printing house and a paper factory in Jerusalem.

222. Interview with Michael Genevisian in Jerusalem, 2022.

223. Under the 1947 Palestine partition plan, the small village of Atlit was located on the Jewish side. Atlit was located 17 kilometers south of Haifa and its inhabitants were fishers or worked in the railway station and prisons built by the British to the east of the village. Atlit's Armenian inhabitants had arrived as refugees in 1920 from Lebanon and settled on land owned by a Christian Arab and leased to the Armenians to farm. See Mustafa Kabaha (2018). *Atlit the City of Salt*. Association of the Defense of the Rights of the Internally Displaced.

224. Statements by interviewees in Mustafa Kabaha (2018), Atlit the City of Salt.

225.   Armenians in the Holy Land celebrate Christmas on the night of January 18
        and Christmas Day is on 19 January.

226.   Interview with Vartouhi Kukeyan in Jerusalem, 2022.

227.   Interviews with David Terzibashian and George Hintlian in Jerusalem, 2022.

228.   Interviews with David Terzibashian in 2021 and 2022. Born as a refugee
        in Amman in 1948 but raised in Jerusalem, he left for the US in 1973 and
        was awarded a master's degree in International Relations and History. He
        worked for Citicorp as an international banker in Dubai, and later as a
        finance manager with AT&T. He is a frequent lecturer on the history of
        Armenians in the Holy Land, specifically in Jerusalem, and the current
        Arab-Israeli conflict.

229.   Institute   of   Palestine   Studies   https://www.palestine-studies.org/en/
        node/78237

230.   Interview with Abcar Zakarian in Jerusalem in 2021 and 2022.

231.   Interview with Alice Zakarian in Jerusalem in 2021 and 2022.

232.   Excerpts from the United Nations Conciliation Commission for Palestine
        Committee on Jerusalem. A summary record of meetings between the
        Committee and the Latin, Armenian and Greek Orthodox Patriarchs of
        Jerusalem (Seventeenth Meeting of the Committee) held in the Old City,
        Jerusalem on 6 April 1949. https://www.un.org/unispal/document/auto-
        insert-211835/. Accessed May 10, 2021.

233.   Christian churches in general owned vast property in the area that became
        Israel. For example, 40% of the land in West Jerusalem was owned by
        Christian churches but all of it fell under Israeli control. Michael Dumper
        in Anthony O'Mahony, editor (1999). *Palestinian Christians: Religion,
        Politics and Society in the Holy Land*, p.59.

234.   Büşra Yalçın (2010). *The Politics of Mainstream Christianity in
        Jerusalem*. History Studies Middle East. Special Issue.

235.   Note from Jirair Tutunjian, 2022.

236.   Silvana was the first company to be incorporated within the Kingdom of
        Jordan at that time. Located in the West Bank town of Ramallah (now in
        the State of Palestine), it produced a variety of products: chocolate, wafers,
        biscuits, gum, and toffees.

237.   The first Palestinian uprising (*intifada* in Arabic) against Israel was 1987-
        1993, the second in the early 2000s. Both *intifadas* had a significant impact

on the Palestinian economy with extended curfews and a detrimental effect on economic conditions.

238. Information from George Hintlian.

239. https://keghart.org/mideasts-first-rocket-remembered/ Mideast's First Rocket Remembered 2011 by Manoug Manougian. Accessed May 10, 2021.

240. Obituary of Hovhannnes S. Donabedian (1924-2021).

241. https://senate.universityofcalifornia.edu/_files/inmemoriam/html/AvedisK.Sanjian.htm and https://oac.cdlib.org/findaid/ark:/13030/c8kh0qpm/

242. https://www.wisdomperiodical.com/index.php/wisdom/article/view/195.

243. https://israelipalestinian.procon.org/source-biographies/haig-khatchadourian/

244. https://armenian-jerusalem.org/literature%20to%20do.htm-Armenian Jerusalem.

245. http://www.armeniapedia.org/wiki/Jerry_Tutunjian.

246. Information from Gabi Kevorkian and George Hintlian in Jerusalem, 2021.

247. The following families are no longer present: Bannayan, Aghabekian, Terzibashian, Babigian, Sultanian, Simonian, Hovsepian, Nercessian, Yeghyaian, Baghsarian, Aprahamian, Chorbajian, Partikian, Bedevian, Soghmonian, and Gazmararian.

248. The families of Genocide survivors who have ceased living in Jerusalem include: Brounsuzian, Iskenderian, Arslanian, Hadjian, Dakessian, Chekijian, Mahserdjian, Katzakhian, Chapadarian, Guvlekjian, Kelekian, Vanayan, Barsamian, Garibian, Kardjian, Haleblian, Atamian, Jambazian, Badigian, and Hovagimian.

249. From Jirair Tutunjian's notes.

250. Varsen Aghabekian and Jamil Rabah. (2017). *Christian Emigration, Displacement and Diaspora* (2017). Published by Diyar. The main reason for pessimism was the instability of the political situation, followed by the deterioration in economic conditions. The most important barriers stated by Christians included difficulties in mobility, restrictions on fundamental freedoms, and economic barriers. The majority believe that the Israeli-Palestinian conflict is turning into a religious conflict.

251. Nancy Kricorian interviewing Ivan Karakashian in *Pursuing Justice in a Culture of Impunity*. (2015).

252. Aghazarian was born in Palestine to Genocide survivors in 1949 and passed away in 2019. He was an eloquent speaker on Palestine and participated

alongside Hanan Ashrawi, the renowned Palestinian spokeswoman, in media activities at the Madrid peace talks. He has written extensively on Armenians in the Holy Land, the Israeli-Palestinian conflict, and the Israeli occupation. His house in the Armenian Quarter was a regular gathering point for journalists and foreigners as his reservoir of knowledge on Jerusalem was unmatched and he was vocal on the Israeli occupation. Excerpt from a NAD/PLO 2019 publication in commemoration of the *Nakba.*

253. See Varsen Aghabekian (2020). *The Double Lockdown: Palestine Under Occupation and COVID-19.* Saeb Erakat and Mitri Raheb editors. Diyar publishers.

254. From Yeghishe Derderian's diary.

References

1. Abel Shifferaw. How Armenian Genocide Survivors Sparked a Revolution in Ethiopian Music. https://www.okayafrica.com/documentary-armenian-modern-ethiopian-music/.

2. Anush Babajanyan (January 5, 2018). https://eurasianet.org/Armenia-community-in-jerusalem-shriks-but-preserves. Accessed January 11, 2021. Jerusalem website

3. Ara Sanjian (2003). The Armenian Church and Community in Jerusalem. In Anthony Mahoney (ed.).The Christian Communities of Jerusalem and the Holy Land: Studies in History, Religion and Politics. Cardiff: University of Wales Press.

4. Armenian Patriarchate of St James Jerusalem website, History, http://www.armenian-patriarchate.org/page2.html.

5. Assadour Antreassian (1969). On Jerusalem and the Armenians.

6. Astrig Tchamkerten (2006). The Gulbenkians in Jerusalem. Calouste Gulbenkian Foundation. Lisbon.

7. Bedross Der Matossian (2021). Armenian Community of Jerusalem: Surviving Against all Odds. CORNERSTONE, Issue 83, Published by Sabeel Ecumenical Liberation Theology Center.

8. Bedross Der Matossian (2018). Armenians of Jerusalem in the modern period: The rise and decline of a community. In Suleiman Mourad, Naoumi Koltun Fromm and Bedross Der Matossian (editors), Routledge Handbook on Jerusalem. Taylor and Francis Group. http://taylorandfrancis.com

9. Bedross Der Matossian (2011). The Armenians of Palestine 1918-48. Faculty Publications, Department of History. 121.https://digitalcommons.unl.edu/historyfacpub/121. Accessed January 11, 2021.

10. Benny Morris (1999). Righteous Victims. Vintage Books, New York.

11. Büşra Yalcin (2010). The Politics of Mainstream Christianity in Jerusalem. History Studies, Middle East. Special Issue.

12. Chapter Fourteen: Destruction and Desecration of Christian Holy Places and Violations of Christian Religious Rights. In Issa Nakhleh (1991). Encyclopedia of the Palestine Problem. Intercontinental Books. New York.

13. Elia Kahvedjian (1995). From the Red Desert to Jerusalem.

14. Emilio Bonfglio and Johannes Preiser-Kapeller (2020). From Ararat to Mount Zion: Armenian Pilgrimage and Presence in the Holy Land, Fourth to Seventh Century. https://books.ub.uni-heidelberg.de/propylaeum/reader/download/711/711-30-89517-1-10-20200702.pdf

15. Garo Sandrouni (2000). On Armenians in Jerusalem.

16. George Hintlian (1998). Fact File: Armenians of Jerusalem. Jerusalem Quarterly File. Issue 2, http://www.jqf-jerusalem.org/journal/1998/jqf2/Armenians.html.

17. Harry Hagopian. The Armenian Church in the Holy Land. http://Armenian-jerusalem.org

18. Harry Hagopian (2002). The Armenian Church in the Holy Land. London. Melisende Publishers.

19. Harutune Mushian (1952). On Jerusalem Hit by Catastrophe.

20. Hoyetchmen's 50th anniversary book. (1937-1987).

21. Hoyetchmen's 70th anniversary book. (1937-2007).

22. Hugh Jones, Reverend. Diary of events May–July 1948. Christ Church, Jerusalem.

23. http://hyeforum.com/index.php?showtopic=32683.

24. https://israelipalestinian.procon.org/source-biographies/haig-khatchadourian/

25. https://armenian-jerusalem.org/literature%20to%20do.htm-Armenian Jerusalem

26. http://www.armeniapedia.org/wiki/Jerry_Tutunjian

27. https://keghart.org/mideasts-first-rocket-remembered/ Mideast's First Rocket Remembered 2011 by Manoug Manougian. Accessed May 10, 2021.

28. https://www.un.org/unispal/document/auto-insert-211835/. Accessed May 10, 2021.

29. https://www.nevo.co.il/law_html/law21/pg-e-0562-2.pdf. Urban property tax ordinances, 1928-1935. Order No.7 of 1936, by the High Commissioner.

30. https://themedialine.org/life-lines-armenian-ceramists-that-changed-the -face-of-Jerusalem

31. https://senate.universityofcalifornia.edu/_files/inmemoriam/html/AvedisK.Sanjian.htm

32. https://oac.cdlib.org/findaid/ark:/13030/c8kh0qpm/

33. https://www.wisdomperiodical.com/index.php/wisdom/article/view/195

34. Institute of Palestine Studies https://www.palestine-studies.org/en/node/78237

35. Janet Abu-Lughod. The Demographic War for Palestine Americans for Middle East Understanding.

36. Jacob Orfali (Hagop Khatcherian) (1987). An Armenian from Jerusalem. Berkeley, CA: Ronin Publishing Inc.

37. James Stocker (Autumn 2017). The United States and the Struggle in the Armenian Patriarchate of Jerusalem 1955-1960. Jerusalem Quarterly 71. https://oldwebsite.palestine-studies.org/jq/issue/71

38. Jirair Tutunjian (2009). Armenian Church in Jerusalem Caught in Palestinian-Israeli Conflict (Part1, II, III). Toronto, https://keghart.org.

39. John Melkon Rose (1993). Armenians of Jerusalem: Memories of Life in Palestine. New York. Radcliffe Press.

40. Keghart. (Sept 2014). Book review by Jirair Tutunjian of *From the Red Desert to Jerusalem* by Elia Kahvedjian.

41. Laury Haytayan. (2011). Armenian Christians in Jerusalem: 1700 Years of Peaceful Presence. Politics and Religion. No 2/2011. Vol. V. pp 179-195.

42. Letter from Africa: Ethiopia's lost Armenian community. (2 March 2020). https://www.bbc.com/news/world-africa-51672965

43. Louis Fishman (2018). The Limitations of Citadinate in Late Ottoman Jerusalem. https://www.jstor.org/stable/10.1163/j.ctvbqs2zk.37. From the book Ordinary Jerusalem, 1840-1940: 'Opening New Archives, Revisiting a Global City by Angelos Dalachanis and Vincent Lemire. Brill Series: Open Jerusalem.

44. LWF-A Heritage of Service 1948-2010. htpps://Jerusalem.lutheranworld.org

45. Maria Chiara Rioli. (2020). Catholic Humanitarian Assistance for Palestinian Refugees in the book Christian Missions and Humanitarianism in the Middle East 1850-1950, edited by Inger Okkenhaug and Karene Summerer. Brill. Pp.253–276. DOI: https://doi.org/10.1163/9789004434530_013

46. Matthew Teller (2022). Nine Quarters of Jerusalem: A New Biography of the Old City. Profile Books.

47. Matthew White (April 2011). Armenian Genocide Survivors in British Mandate Palestine: A Social History.

48. Manachem Kline (2014). Lives in Common: Arabs and Jews in Jerusalem, Jaffa, and Hebron. Oxford University Press.

49. Michael Dumper in Anthony O'Mahony, editor (1999). Palestinian Christians: Religion, Politics and Society in the Holy Land. Melisende. London.

50. Michelle U Compos. (2011). Ottoman Brothers: Muslims, Christians and Jews in Early Twentieth Century Palestine. Stanford, California. Stanford University Press.

51. Mustafa Kabaha (2018). Atlit the City of Salt. Association of the Defense of the Rights of the Internally Displaced.

52. Nancy Kricorian. (2015). Pursuing Justice in a Culture of Impunity: Ivan Karakashian of Defense for Children International Palestine. January 22, 2015. https://armenianweekly.com/2015/01/22/karakashian-palestine/

53. Nathan Krystall (1999). The Fall of the New City, 1947-1950. In Jerusalem 1948: The Arab Neighborhoods and their Fate in the War. Salim Tamari (editor). Institute of Jerusalem Studies and Badil Resource Center, pp.92-153.

54. Nora Arsenian Carmi. (2021). We are Still Here. CORNERSTONE. Issue 83. Published by Sabeel Ecumenical Liberation Theology Center.

55. Razmig Panossian (2006). The Armenians: From Kings and Priests to Merchants and Commissars. New York: Columbia University Press.

56. Rev. Fr. Pakrad Bourjekian. (2013). The Mamluk Inscription of the St. James Armenian Monastery Inside the Armenian Quarter of the Old City, Jerusalem. Journal of the Society for Armenian Studies, pp.239-251.

57. Rochelle Davis (1999). The Growth of Western Communities, 1917-1948. In Jerusalem 1948: The Arab Neighborhoods and their Fate in the War. Salim Tamari (editor). Institute of Jerusalem Studies and Badil Resource Center, pp.32-73.

58. Rochelle Davis (2015). Growing up Palestinian in Jerusalem before 1948: Childhood Memories of Communal Life, Education, and Political Awareness. Book chapter in Jerusalem Interrupted: Modernity and Colonial Transformation 1917-Present, edited by Lena Jayyusi. Interlink Publishers, pp.187-210.

59. Salim Tamari (Summer 2014). Issa Al Issa's Unorthodoxy: Banned in Jerusalem, Permitted in Jaffa. In Jerusalem Quarterly.

60. Salim Tamari (2000). Jerusalem's Ottoman Modernity: The Times and Lives of Wasif Jawhariyyeh. In Jerusalem Quarterly No.9.

61. Salman Abu Sittah (2011). Palestine Atlas. Palestine Land Society. London.

62. Yeghishe Derderian. Diary published in the Almanac of the Armenian Patriarchate of Jerusalem.

63. Sa'eed Ammouri. (2020). Armenians in Jerusalem's History: Armenian Palestinian is How They Define Themselves. Https:raseef22.net/article.

64. Samuel J Kuruvilla. The Politics of Mainstream Christianity in Jerusalem (2010). History Studies. Middle East Special Issue 2010.

65. Sato Moughalian (2019). Feast of Ashes: The Life and Art of David Ohannessian. Stanford University Press.

66. Seth J. Frantzman. (Thesis 2006). Identity and Inclination: The Arab Christians Between Zionism and Islam. Hebrew University.

67. Sion. (1948 and 1949). Publication of the Armenian Patriarchate of Jerusalem. Editor-Father Hagop Vartanian. Printed by the Armenian Convent Printing Press. Jerusalem, Palestine.

68. Sossie Andézian. (2017). A New Ethno-Religious Entity in British Mandate Palestine: The Armenian Catholic Community. journals.openedition.org. https://doi.org/10.4000/eac.1117. Accessed February 16, 2021.

69. Sylva Natalie Manoogian (2013). The Calouste Gulbenkian Library, Armenian Patriarchate of Jerusalem, 1925-1990: An Historical Portrait of a Monastic and Lay Community Intellectual Resource Center. A dissertation submitted in partial satisfaction of the requirements for the degree Doctor of Philosophy in Library and Information Science. University of California, LA.

70. Tania Manougian (2007). The Armenian Community in the Holy Land. This Week in Palestine of 30 July 2007.

71. The Diaries of Constantine Mavrides, May 15-December 30, 1948. Memoranda 1-5. An appendix in Jerusalem 1948: The Arab Neighborhoods and Their Fate in the War. Salim Tamari (editor), Institute of Palestine Studies and Badil Resource Center, pp.262-277.

72. This Week in Palestine. Issue 225. May 2022. Life in Pre-1948 Jerusalem. www.thisweekinpalestine.com

73. Unpublished paper in Arabic titled "The Arab Christian Palestinians in Gaza: I was with them."

74. Varsen Aghabekian (2021). A Palestinian Armenian: The Intertwine between the Social and the Political. Dar Al Kalima University Press.

75. Varsen Aghabekian (2020). The Double Lockdown: Palestine under Occupation and COVID-19. Saeb Erakat and Mitri Raheb editors. Diyar publishers.

76. Varsen Aghabekian and Jamil Rabah. (2017). Palestinian Christians: Emigration, Displacement and Diaspora. Diyar publishers.

77. Victor Azarya (1984). The Armenian Quarter of Jerusalem. Urban Life Behind Monastery Walls. Berkeley, CA: University of California Press.

78. Vincent Lemire. (2017). Jerusalem 1900. The Holy City in the Age of Possibilities. Chicago University Press.

79. www.paljourneys.org Palestine Photographers before 1948: Palestine Journey. Accessed January 15, 2021.

80. Zachary J. Foster. (2011). Arab Historiography in Mandatory Palestine 1920-1948. A thesis submitted to the Faculty of the Graduate School of Arts and Sciences of Georgetown University in partial fulfillment of the requirements for the degree of Master of Arts Studies. Washington, DC.

Index

A

About the Author

Varsen Aghabekian

Holder of a Ph.D. from the University of Pittsburgh/US and a management and policy consultant. Teaches and consults at Dar al-Kalima University. Dr. Aghabekian has directed several national studies and authored numerous manuals, articles, and national reports on Jerusalem, education, youth, and women. Recent publications include topics such as Palestinian women in politics, Christian migration from the Holy Land, and A Palestinian Armenian: The Intertwine between the Social and the Political. She is a founding member of several non-governmental organizations, and an active member of university boards and human rights organizations. She served as the Commissioner General of the Palestinian Independent Commission for Human Rights, is a member of the Presidential Committee for the Restoration of the Church of the Nativity, and a member of the Presidential Committee on Church Affairs. Dr. Aghabekian is married and has three children and two granddaughters. She can be contacted on Varsen2003@yahoo.com.

Made in the USA
Las Vegas, NV
05 February 2025

17610617R00125